The Continuing Challenge:

The Past and the Future of

Brown v. Board of Education

The Continuing Challenge:

The Past and
The Future of
Brown v. Board of Education

A Symposium

Published for
Notre Dame Center for Civil Rights
Notre Dame, Indiana
Integrated Education Associates
Evanston, Illinois

Published by Integrated Education Associates
2003 Sheridan Road
Evanston, Illinois 60201
Library of Congress Catalog Card No. 75-1552
International Standard Book No. 912008-09-01
Manufactured in the United States

The article by Arthur J. Goldberg included in this book has previously appeared in an edited form as "Reflections: Twentieth Anniversary of *Brown v. Board of Education*," 50 *Notre Dame Lawyer* 106 (1974). Reprinted with permission. © 1974 by the *Notre Dame Lawyer*, University of Notre Dame.

Contents

Foreword . . . . *Howard A. Glickstein* ix

REFLECTIONS ON *BROWN V. BOARD OF EDUCATION*

Implications of *Brown* . . . . *Phineas Indritz* 1
Twenty Years Later . . . . *Constance Baker Motley* 11
Delaware's Contribution to *Brown* . . *Louis L. Redding* 25

ISSUES OF OUR TIME

Speeding Reforms . . . . *Joseph B. Robison* 31
Segregation Based on Language . . . . *José A. Cabranes* 37
The Post-*Brown* Decades . . . . *Richard G. Hatcher* 43
The Emerging Meanings of Equal
  Educational Opportunities . . . . . . *David L. Kirp* 47
Outlook for the Future . . . . *Brian K. Landsberg* 51
A New Look at *Brown* . . . . *Ruby G. Martin* 55
Chicanos and Equal
  Educational Opportunity . . . . *Vilma S. Martinez* 59
Desegregation at Midpoint . . . . *Gary Orfield* 65
An Appeal for Unity . . . . *Arthur J. Goldberg* 75

THE CONTINUING CHALLENGE

The Message of *Brown*
  for White America . . . . *Theodore M. Hesburgh, C.S.C.* . . . 81

Bibliography 87

Editor's Note:

Two important cases discussed in the following articles were awaiting decision by the Supreme Court at the time of the Center for Civil Rights' Conference on March 21 and 22, 1974. The Supreme Court has now announced its decision in both cases. In *DeFunis v. Odegaard,* 416 U.S. 312 (1974), the Court held that the case was moot and, therefore, reached no decision on the issue of whether the University of Washington could constitutionally take the race or national origin of minority applicants into account in determining admission to law school. In *Milliken V. Bradley,* ___U.S.___ 94 S. Ct. 3112, (1974), the Court, in a 5-to-4 decision rejected a metropolitan school desegregation plan for Detroit and its suburbs. Although the Court's majority found no justification in the facts of the case for a remedy crossing school district lines, it did not rule out such a remedy entirely. A metropolitan remedy might be appropriate, in the Court's view, if school district lines had been drawn or manipulated to segregate students or if illegal segregation within one district had had a substantial impact on neighboring districts.

Contributors

Howard A. Glickstein, Director of the Center for Civil Rights at the University of Notre Dame.

Phineas Indritz, Counsel to the Subcommittee on Conservation and Natural Resources of the House of Representatives Committee on Government Operations.

Constance Baker Motley, United States District Court Judge for the Southern District of New York.

Louis L. Redding, an attorney in private practice in Wilmington, Delaware.

Joseph B. Robison, Director of the Commission on Law, Social Action and Urban Affairs of the American Jewish Congress.

José A. Cabranes, Administrator of the Washington Office of the Commonwealth of Puerto Rico.

Richard G. Hatcher, Mayor of Gary, Indiana.

David L. Kirp, Professor in the Graduate School of Public Policy at the University of California, Berkeley.

Brian K. Landsberg, Chief, Education Section, Civil Rights Division, United States Department of Justice.

Ruby G. Martin, Counsel to the Committee on the District of Columbia of the U.S. House of Representatives and codirector of the Washington Research Project.

Contributors

Vilma S. Martinez, General Counsel of the Mexican American Legal Defense and Educational Fund.

Gary Orfield, Research Associate The Brookings Institution.

Arthur J. Goldberg, former Supreme Court Justice in private law practice in Washington, D.C.

Theodore M. Hesburgh, president of The University of Notre Dame and a charter member of the U.S. Commission on Civil Rights.

Foreword

On May 17, 1954, the Supreme Court announced its historic decision in *Brown v. Board of Education.* In the twenty tumultous years since that day, the decision has become not only a landmark in the development of American jurisprudence but also a leading force in all aspects of our nation's recent social development. *Brown* declared that separate educational facilities for minorities were inherently unequal. In subsequent decisions, the Court quickly struck down other aspects of the Jim Crow apartheid which characterized so much of American life. *Brown's* impact, however, goes beyond racial issues; it has brought alive once again those guarantees of fundamental rights and equality embodied in the Fourteenth Amendment. It has served, and continues to serve, as the foundation for our quest for equal justice in the Untied States.

On March 21 and 22, 1974, the Notre Dame Center for Civil Rights conducted a two-day conference to commemorate the twentieth anniversary of the *Brown* decision. This conference, entitled *Brown v. Board of Education: Reflections on the Continuing Challenge,* was the first in a series of annual conferences the Center will conduct on an issue or issues of concern to the civil rights movement. The Center, established in 1973 by a grant from the Ford Foundation, is a resource for research on civil rights history. It analyzes current civil rights issues and makes recommendations to meet contemporary civil rights problems. The Center is also a resource for educators and scholars at the University.

In part the Center's first conference looked to the past to reflect on the controversies surrounding the decision and the history of its implementation.

But for the greater part, the conference looked to the present and to the future to consider how best to meet the continuing challenge of providing equal educational opportunity to all.

The first day of the conference consisted of presentations by individuals who had played important roles in the Supreme Court's consideration of *Brown v. Board of Education* twenty years ago. As a young attorney for the NAACP Legal Defense and Education Fund, the Honorable Constance Baker Motley, now United States District judge for the Southern District of New York, participated in preparing the briefs filed in the *Brown* case. Judge Motley discusses the NAACP strategies, the tragic effects of the Supreme Court's decision to require only gradual implementation of its decree, and the diminishing direct relevance of the decision for the high concentrations of blacks in New York City and other major metropolitan areas. Phineas Indritz, currently counsel to a Subcommittee of the House of Representatives Committee on Government Operations, filed a brief in *Brown* on behalf of the American Veterans Committee. His article considers the social and legal history building up to *Brown,* the use of *Brown* to strike down segregation in other areas of American life, and the relevance of *Brown* to major issues before the Supreme Court at the time of the conference. Louis L. Redding, an attorney from Wilmington, Delaware, and Joseph B. Robison, Director of the Commission on Law, Social Action and Urban Affairs of the American Jewish Congress, present particularized views on the *Brown* decision. Mr. Redding, who represented black Delaware children in a companion case to *Brown,* discusses his personal involvement in the case as the first black attorney in that state. Joseph B. Robison, who filed a brief in *Brown* on behalf of the American Jewish Congress, pays particular attention to the relationship between the case and its gradual implementation, and our efforts to achieve integrated housing.

The second day of the conference concentrated on contemporary educational issues. The panel of distinguished commentators was comprised of Jose A. Cabranes, Administrator of the Washington Office of the Commonwealth of Puerto Rico; the Honorable Richard G. Hatcher, Mayor of Gary, Indiana; David L. Kirp, Professor at the University of California at Berkeley; Ruby G. Martin, Counsel to the Committee on the District of Columbia of the House of Representatives; Vilma S. Martinez, General Counsel of the Mexican American Legal Defense and Educational Fund; Gary Orfield, Research Associate at the Brookings Institution, and Brian K. Landsberg, Chief, Education Section of the Civil Rights Division of the Department of Justice. The panelists' presentations as set forth in the following pages comprise a lively interchange on such issues as busing, the continuing validity of integration as a predominant goal in the search for quality education and bilingual education.

The addresses delivered at the Conference by the Honorable Arthur J. Goldberg, former Associate Justice of the United States Supreme Court, and the Reverend Theodore M. Hesburgh, C.S.C., President of the University of Notre Dame and former Chairman of the United States Commission on Civil Rights, are also included here. Justice Goldberg discusses the cynicism of the Watergate era and its effect on the civil rights movement. He urges us to reaffirm our commitment to the principles enunciated in *Brown* and to reestablish the basic political coalitions that have been threatened by controversies over quotas and related issues. Justice Goldberg also expresses his hope that the Supreme Court will unite, as it did in the Warren era, to insure that we continue to progress toward equal justice for all. Father Hesburgh discusses another aspect of the *Brown* decision and the civil rights movement— its importance to white Americans. He states that in a pluralistic society all of us, white, brown and black, are damaged if we live in racial isolation. He urges white Americans to realize the great benefits they have received from the civil rights movement and to push forward to achieve *Brown's* promise of equality.

The Center for Civil Rights was greatly assisted by the efforts of many individuals in preparing for this First Annual Conference and the publication of its proceedings. We would like to thank in particular Marian Wright Edelman, Director of the Children's Defense Fund; M. Carl Holman, President of the National Urban Coalition; Grace Olivarez, Director of the Institute for Social Research and Development at the University of New Mexico; Oscar Garcia-Rivera, Chairman of Aspira of New York, Inc.; William L. Taylor, Director of the Center for National Policy Review—all of whom serve as members of the National Advisory Council of the Center for Civil Rights—and Professor Francis X. Beytagh of the Notre Dame Law School. Their efforts as moderators and speakers greatly enriched the conference. In addition, a special tribute is due to the dedicated staff of the Center and the many persons associated with the University who worked so tirelessly to insure the success of the conference. Finally, we would like to express our appreciation to Meyer Weinberg, Editor of *Integrated Education,* and Gertrude Martin, its Managing Editor. Their patient efforts and cooperation have made possible the publication of these pages.

Howard A. Glickstein
Director of the Center for Civil Rights
Notre Dame, Indiana

Implications of *Brown*

Phineas Indritz

We assemble today, almost twenty years after the United States Supreme Court's decisions in the Public School Segregation Cases, to reflect on their place in history and to meditate on their consequences and future.

Those decisions declared that racial segregation in public schools violate the Equal Protection clause of the Fourteenth Amendment (in the states)[1] and the Due Process clause of the Fifth Amendment (in the federal territory of the District of Columbia).[2] They were hailed throughout the world as a victory for human freedom and equality. That, indeed, was true. They clearly told the country that the "separate but equal" doctrine—which since 1896 had been the legal fiction used to justify governmentally-imposed racial segregation—was no longer viable in the courts.

But these decisions did not stand alone. They were the culmination of four developments which had been going on for some time in the world, in our country, and in the courts:

World War II and the horrors of Hitler's racism had profoundly sharpened America's insight into the evils of race discrimination. Large numbers of citizen soldiers found that racial segregation made no sense when facing the enemy, in the mud and the foxholes, or in the battles at sea. They returned with a keener awareness of the similarity between our racism at home and the evils they fought against in that global war.

The hurts and degradation which legally enforced racism imposed on both whites and Negroes and on our entire country were being analyzed in a series of monumental studies which were widely publicized. Some of these were:

1

Gunnar Myrdal, *An American Dilemma, The Negro Problem and Modern Democracy* (1944);
Report of the Fair Employment Practices Committee (1946);
President Truman's June 29, 1947 speech at the Lincoln Memorial, 93 Cong. Rec. A-3505;
Report ("To Secure These Rights") of President Truman's Committee on Civil Rights (1947);
Report ("Segregation in Washington") by the privately sponsored National Committee on Segregation in the Nation's Capital (1948);
Report ("Freedom to Serve") by President Truman's Committee on Equality of Treatment and Opportunity in the Armed Services, under the chairmanship of Judge Charles Fahy (1950).

The half dozen years following the end of World War II had seen a remarkable dropping of racial barriers throughout the country—in the South as well as the North—except where those barriers were specifically required by law.

These changes occurred in public and private schools and colleges; in public accommodations such as libraries, theaters, department stores, bus terminals, hotels, playgrounds, hospitals, golf courses, swimming pools, restaurants and airports; in associations of doctors, nurses, educators, lawyers, scientists and others; in councils and boards of religious bodies; in professional and collegiate athletics; in concert halls and on the stage.

Everywhere the old order of exclusion and segregation was giving way to acceptance on merit rather than skin color. These changes did not occur easily or automatically. Often they came only after great controversy and travail. But they proved that desegregation works—that after the initial controversy, desegregation results in less rather than more violence—that the abolition of racial barriers improves the community and reduces the burden on the dignity and spirit of all people, white, black, pink or brown.

In almost every instance of such desegregation, the very fact of the struggle and the accomplishment laid the groundwork for desegregation in other instances.

Finally legal research by civil rights attorneys had begun to assemble the facts, arguments and precedents showing that the foundations for the "separate but equal" doctrine were quite inconsistent with many Supreme Court decisions that had repudiated racial segregation in various facets of our national life. These included:

Housing and Land Occupancy
  Buchanan v. Warley, 245 U.S. 60 (1917)
  Shelley v. Kraemer and *Hurd v. Hodge,* 334 U.S. 1, 24 (1948)
Employment
  Yick Wo v. Hopkins, 118 U.S. 356 (1886)
  Steele v. Louisville & Nashville R. Co., 323 U.S. 192 (1944)
Education
  Missouri ex rel. Gaines v. Canada, 305 U.S. 337 (1938)
  Sipuel v. Board of Regents, 332 U.S. 631 (1948)
  Sweatt v. Painter, 339 U.S. 629 (1950)

McLaurin v. Oklahoma State Regents, 339 U.S. 637 (1950)
Transportation
    Mitchell v. United States, 313 U.S. 80 (1941)
    Henderson v. United States, 339 U.S. 816 (1950)
    Railroad Co. v. Brown, 84 U.S. (17 Wall.) 445 (1873)
Jury Service
    Strauder v. West Virginia, 100 U.S. 303 (1880)
    Virginia v. Rives, 100 U.S. 313 (1880)
    Ex parte Virginia 100 U.S. 339 (1880)
    Cassell v. Texas, 339 U.S. 282 (1950)

In all of these cases, the person claiming violation of his or her constitutional right could attain it only if there were no racial segregation. In each of these cases the Supreme Court ruled that he or she was entitled to the constitutional right and could not be deprived of it under the guise of racial "separation".

By 1950, the legal foundation for the grand assault on the "separate but equal" doctrine had been fully established by four major Supreme Court decisions which, though couched in the language of "discrimination", had defined the issue in a way that eliminated every effective distinction between discrimination and segregation, and made segregation a form of unconstitutional discrimination. These were:

1. The evisceration of racial restrictive housing covenants in 1948 by *Shelley v. Kraemer.*

2. *Sweatt v. Painter,* where Texas created a separate law school for Sweatt in response to his effort to enroll in the University of Texas Law School. But the Supreme Court did not simply compare the physical facilities of the two schools to ascertain the claimed "equality". "What is more important," the Court emphasized, are the "qualities which are incapable of objective measurement," such as "standing in the community, traditions and prestige" and the factors of "isolation" and "academic vacuum, removed from the interplay of ideas and the exchange of views" with the dominant majority.[3]

3. In *McLaurin v. Oklahoma State Regents,* the University of Oklahoma admitted McLaurin to its graduate school and eventually let him use "the same classroom, library and cafeteria as students of other races." The University insisted only on assigning him to a seat or a table designated for "colored" students.[4] The Supreme Court ruled that setting McLaurin "apart from the other students" would "impair and inhibit his ability to study, to engage in discussions and exhange views with other students", and hence was unconstitutional.[5]

4. In *Henderson v. United States,* the Supreme Court ruled that the

3

Interstate Commerce Act's prohibition against "undue or unreasonable . . . disadvantage" (which the Court interpreted in light of the 14th Amendment's Equal Protection Clause) was violated when the Southern Railway segregated Elmer Henderson at the end table behind a green curtain in the railroad's dining car.

It is true that the Court's *Sweatt, McLaurin* and *Henderson* opinions said that it did not "need" to "reach petitioner's contention that *Plessy v. Ferguson* should be reexamined in the light of contemporary knowledge respecting the purposes of the Fourteenth Amendment and the effects of racial segregation."[6] But the Court's insistence on the individual's "personal and present" right to the "same treatment", regardless of race, in the context of the intangible and psychological factors involved in those cases, demonstrated that the *Plessy* doctrine had come to the brink of its grave.

I believe it is fair to say that without these foundation stones, the results of the 1954 Public School Segregation Cases would have been very different.

There are several reasons why the 1954 decisions were far more dramatic than the earlier decisions:

The earlier rulings tended to be stated in terms of "discrimination" without clearly facing the truth that racial separation enforced by law can never provide equality and always results in unequal facilities for minority peoples.

The earlier rulings generally applied to a few persons. At that time, few Negroes served on juries, went to law or other graduate schools, or ate in railroad dining cars. The 1954 rulings, however, involved elementary, junior and senior high schools, and the press created a nation-wide awareness that the decisions would affect virtually all the public schools in the South and border states with their hundreds of thousands of pupils and the emotions and fears of millions of parents and other relatives.

The importance of the cases was emphasized by the fact the the Supreme Court, after hearing argument in 1952, set the cases for reargument on five questions in the 1953 Term, and after its May 17, 1954 decisions, ordered another re-argument on the form of the decrees before issuing them in 1955.[7] This procedure heightened national interest and suspense in a manner not equaled until the Court's recent decisions in the abortion cases.[8]

The Court underscored the importance of its rulings by issuing a unanimous opinion remarkable for its clarity and simplicity—which the entire country could readily understand. The *Brown* opinion squarely stated that it was directed against the principle of racial segregation itself, "even though the physical facilities and other 'tangible' factors may be equal".[9] Whatever doubt remained as to the Court's intention to destroy the "separate but equal" doctrine was dissipated the following Monday, when the Court decided six more cases involving undergraduate university and college education,[10] golf courses,[11] public housing,[12] and a municipal amphitheatre.[13] In three of these cases, the Court denied petitions for certiorari where the lower courts had ruled against racial segregation. In the other three cases, where the lower courts had upheld racial distinctions, the Court granted the petitions and remanded the cases for reconsideration in light of the Public School Segregation decisions of May 17

The 1954 decisions greatly accelerated the crumbling of the walls of racial segregation. They catalyzed a nationwide reexamination, reevaluation, modification and abandonment of the previous legal and traditional patterns of segregation by race. In many instances the changes occurred rapidly, with voluntary acceptance. In other instances, the change was much slower, as the defenders of segregation fought to maintain the *status quo* or to capitalize on the "deliberate" rather than the "speed" in the Court's 1955 formula of "with all deliberate speed". They resorted to every obstructive and delaying tactic that ingenious, determined and stubborn enemies of freedom could devise including "massive resistance", "interposition", gerrymandering of school boundaries, violence and other extra-legal pressures, legislative investigations, persecution of civil rights organizations, closing of schools and other public facilities to avoid desegregation, community inertia, drawn out litigation, and misuse of public funds to finance other devices to evade or delay integration.

The 1954 decisions did not end *de facto* segregation. But by knocking out the "separate but equal"underpinning of governmentally enforced racial segregation, they set the stage for a fundamental revolution in our laws and social patterns. Previously we had to fight against laws *requiring* racial discrimination. The 1954 decisions enabled us to turn our attention to the enactment and enforcement of laws *prohibiting* racial discrimination.[14]

The 1954 decisions were thus the foundation stones for the Civil Rights Acts of 1957, 1960, 1964, 1965, 1968 and 1972. On this foundation, the Commission on Civil Rights, established by the 1957 Act, developed the data and published the reports which laid the essential groundwork for a steady stream of legislative and administrative efforts to end racial discrimination in our nation. These Civil Rights laws gave life to the Fifteenth Amendment's prohibition against race discrimination in voting; and prohibited discrimination in places of public accommodation and in the expenditure of public

5

funds in housing, schools, hospitals, and many other areas of community activity; and established the Equal Employment Opportunity Commission to foster nondiscrimination in employment. These laws and the resulting court decisions have firmly set our nation's policy on the road toward the eventual end of racism.

The journey over the past twenty years has not been easy, nor has it been as fast or as successful as we had hoped, or as it ought to have been. We are still fighting the battles of widespread discrimination in employment. The recent efforts to enact anti-busing legislation in Congress, both in the Education bill and in the Energy Emergency bill, sharply remind us that the battle against racially discriminatory legislation is still too much with us.

Nor have we yet completed the constitutional battles over the place of race in our national life. Every Term of Court has seen new judicial decisions refining the issues and the extent of judicial remedy against race discrimination:

Miscegenation Laws
  Loving v. Virginia, 388 U.S. 1 (1967);
Housing
  Reitman v. Mulkey, 387 U.S. 369 (1967);
  Jones v. Alfred H. Mayer Co., 392 U.S. 409 (1968);
  Hunter v. Erickson, 393 U.S. 385 (1969);
  Trafficante v. Metropolitan Life Insurance Co., 409 U.S. 205 (1972);
Recreational Facilities
  Sullivan v. Little Hunting Park, 396 U.S. 229 (1969);
  Tillman v. Wheaton Haven Recreation Association, 410 U.S. 431 (1973);
Schools
  Griffin v. Prince Edward School Board, 377 U.S. 218 (1964);
  Green v. County School Board, 391 U.S. 430 (1968);
  Raney v. Board of Education, 391 U.S. 443 (1968);
  U.S. v. Montgomery County Board of Education, 395 U.S. 225 (1969);
  Alexander v. Holmes County Board of Education, 396 U.S. 19 (1969);
  Northcross v. Memphis School Board, 397 U.S. 232 (1970);
  Swann v. Charlotte-Mecklenburg County Board of Education, 402 U.S. 1 (1971);
  Wright v. Council of Emporia, 407 U.S. 451 (1972);
  U.S. v. Scotland Neck Board of Education, 407 U.S. 484 (1972).

Most of these decisions have helped strengthen the principle enunciated 78 years ago by the first Mr. Justice Harlan in his immortal dissent in *Plessy v. Ferguson.*[15] ". . . Our Constitution is color-blind, and neither knows nor tolerates classes among citizens. In respect of civil rights, all citizens are equal before the law."

It is regrettable that a few decisions have run counter to that trend, such as *Evans v. Abney,*[16] and *Moose Lodge No. 107 v. Irvis.*[17]

Two sets of cases are now pending before the Supreme Court which test the direction in which we are now travelling.

In the *Detroit School* cases[18] the pupils in the city schools are seventy-five percent black, while in the surrounding suburban schools the pupils are over ninety-eight percent white. The lower courts ruled that the school districts, as subordinate units of the state which has basic responsibility for public education compatible with the Constitution, must end the school segregation on a metropolitan basis and across the existing school district lines, rather than only within the City of Detroit.

The U.S. Justice Department argues, as it did in the Richmond, Virginia school case, on which the Supreme Court divided 4-4 last year,[19] that remedies for unconstitutional school segregation may extend beyond the boundaries of a single school district only if, and to the extent that, unconstitutional acts of segregation have directly altered or substantially affected the racial composition of schools in more than one school district.

It seems to me that the state has responsibility for providing unsegregated public education;[20] that school districts are subordinate agencies of the state; and that if racial segregation occurs in a metropolitan area, the state has the responsibility to alter its school boundary lines, or to make other appropriate arrangements to terminate the racial segregation. A more difficult case would be one involving school districts across state lines, such as the District of Columbia whose pupil population is largely black and is surrounded by Virginia and Maryland with largely white pupil populations.

The case of *DeFunis v. Odegaard*,[21] is much more difficult: May a State agency use race as the basis for discriminating in favor of persons of minority groups and against a person of the majority group, by rejecting the application for admission into a state law school of a person of the majority group while admitting persons of minority groups with lesser qualifications?

In this case, the University of Washington Law School received 1,601 applications for admission to 150 openings. It divided the applicants into two groups—one consisting of black Americans, Chicano Americans, American Indians and Philippine Americans. The other group consisted of all others—whites, Chinese, Japanese or other Asian Americans, foreigners, etc. Their qualifications were compared separately. Forty-four minority applicants were accepted, thirty-eight of whom apparently scored less on the Predicted First-Year Average formula used by the law school than did DeFunis, a white applicant who was not accepted. (Of the forty-four minority applicants accepted, eighteen actually enrolled.) DeFunis sued, claiming he was denied admittance to law school solely on the basis of racial discrimination.

The case has become the forum for a major conflict among those of us dedicated to the advancement of civil rights. Long-established friends and allies in the civil rights struggle are arrayed on opposite sides, each making extreme arguments.

One side contends that it is constitutionally required, or at least permissible on a "voluntary" basis, to give preference, on the basis of race, to persons of minority groups at the expense of those not from a minority group. The other side maintains that the Constitution prohibits a state agency from using race as the sole basis for giving preferred treatment to some persons over others.

Both sides apparently agree on the propriety of "affirmative action" which assists disadvantaged students in overcoming cultural or economic handicaps, which seeks to recruit in areas and institutions where minority students are present, or which provides special educational preparation to the scholastically handicapped, both before and during school attendance.

Those who support the university say that the Court's decisions against race as a constitutional criterion must be read in light of the fact that most of them involved actions *discriminating against* blacks or other minorities, and hence did not invalidate using race as a criterion for *benefitting* them. On the other hand, the Supreme Court has said that rules of selection must be based on qualifications without regard to race, religion, sex or national origin, and without "discriminatory preference for any groups, minority or majority",[22] and must be "fair and racially neutral".[23]

Those who support the university also argue that the state must discriminate on the basis of race in order to rectify past discriminations against minority groups. On the other hand, those who oppose the university point out:

- that there is no evidence that the university discriminated in the past;
- that the percentage of its minority students is about the same as the percentage of such minorities in the Pacific Northwest;
- that the burden of the discrimination falls on individuals who did not themselves discriminate and who, in fact, may themselves be relatively disadvantaged;
- that the university's criterion of race was based on the assumption that all persons of the minority groups suffered actual cultural or economic deprivation and the university made no effort to ascertain whether that was true for the particular individuals;
- that such assumption reinforces invidious stereotypes that all persons of the minority groups are inferior and unqualified.

This case poses a particularly sensitive problem for the Court. A broadly phrased opinion, either way, could have disastrous consequences. On the one hand, it might hinder the desegregation process in higher education and in employment under the affirmative remedial measures required by the federal government. On the other hand, to establish race as a constitutionally permissible criterion for judging individual merit may in the long run reestablish much of the color-line spirit of *Plessy v. Ferguson,* and make the individual less meritorious than his or her ancestry.

Ironically, this case does not require the Court to venture into this dilemma. Since at least fifty-five other "majority" persons were ahead of DeFunis on the waiting list, it is questionable whether he would have been reached even if none of the eighteen minority persons had been admitted. Furthermore, this case is virtually moot. It is not a class action or suit to enjoin future use of the challenged procedure, but involves only DeFunis, who was admitted after he filed the suit and will graduate in June 1974.

Whatever the Court does, I hope it will avoid the pitfalls of an overbroad ruling, while continuing to advance the promise of *Brown v. Broad of Education.*

[1] *Brown v. Board of Education,* 347 U.S. 483 (May 17, 1954).

[2] *Bolling v. Sharpe,* 347 U.S. 497 (May 17, 1954).

[3] 339 U.S. at 634.

[4] 339 U.S. at 640.

[5] Ibid. at 641.

[6] 339 U.S. at 631; 339 U.S. at 638; 339 U.S. at 826.

[7] 349 U.S. 294 (1955).

[8] *Roe v. Wade,* 410 U.S. 113 (1973); *Doe v. Bolton,* 410 U.S. 179 (1973).

[9] 347 U.S. at 493.

[10] *State of Florida ex rel. Hawkins v. Board of Control,* 347 U.S. 971 (Florida); *Tureaud v. Board of Supervisors,* 347 U.S. 971 (Louisiana); *Wichita Falls Jr. College v. Battle,* 347 U.S. 974 (Texas).

[11] *Holcombe v. Beal,* 347 U.S. 974 (Texas).

[12] *Housing Authority of San Francisco v. Banks,* 347 U.S. 974 (California).

[13] *Muir v. Louisville Park Theatrical Association,* 347 U.S. 971 (Kentucky).

[14] *District of Columbia v. John R. Thompson Co.,* 346 U.S. 100 (1953).

[15] 163 U.S. 537, 559 (1896).

[16] 396 U.S. 435 (1970).

[17] 407 U.S. 163 (1972).

[18] *Milliken v. Bradley,* No. 73-434; *Allen Park Public Schools District v. Bradley,* No. 73-435; *The Grosse Pointe Public School System v. Bradley,* No. 73-436.

[19] *Bradley v. School Board of City of Richmond, VA,* 338 F. Supp. 67, reversed 462 F. 2d 1058 (CA 4), affirmed by equally divided Court *sub nom. School Board of City of Richmond v. State Board of Education,* 412 U.S. 92 (1973).

[20] *Brown,* 347 U.S. 483, 493 (1954) which said that "education is perhaps the most important function of state and local governments," and *San Antonio Independent School District v. Rodriguez,* 411 U.S. 1, 35-37 (1973) which said that education is not "a fundamental right or liberty" entitled to constitutional protection.

[21] No. 73-235.

[22] *Griggs v. Duke Power Co.,* 401 U.S. 424, 431 (1971).

[23] *McDonnell Douglas Corp. v. Green,* 411 U.S. 792, 801 (1973).

Twenty Years Later...

Constance Baker Motley

When the Supreme Court announced its decision in 1954 barring state-enforced racial segregation in education that was only one part of its historic decision. The more difficult second part was yet to come. In that May 17, 1954 decision the Court directed counsel for both sides to submit new briefs in answer to questions 4 and 5. These questions dealt with the type of relief to which petitioners would be entitled. The five cases were also set down for further arguments as to these questions.[1] As far as counsel for petitioners were concerned that directive fell on a stunned, physically and mentally exhausted crew of so-called civil rights lawyers.

The five cases, which are collectively referred to here as *Brown,* were first argued before the Supreme Court in December 1952. On June 8, 1953, after initial arguments, the Court had set the cases down for reargument. In an order issued at that time the Court propounded to counsel five multi-part questions. Three of the questions dealt with substantive constitutional issues and two dealt with the type of relief to be afforded should the petitioners prevail.[2] We all had the feeling then that we were about to embark upon momentous times.

Following the June 8, 1953 order, National Association for the Advancement of Colored People (NAACP) Legal Defense Fund (LDF) lawyers operated on a seven-day work week schedule. Months of research, conferences, and debate involving historians, sociologists, legal scholars and lawyers culminated in the memorable 235-page brief and appendix filed in September 1953. We, therefore, found the 1954 order for further briefs and arguments after two prior briefs and arguments incredible.

11

I left the victory party in our New York City offices on the evening of May 17, 1954 to fill a speaking engagement a day or so later in Selma, Alabama. Walter White, then Executive Secretary of the NAACP, had become ill and was unable to keep the scheduled speaking engagement in Selma. He asked me to go in his place. Upon arrival in Selma, I was shocked to find no rejoicing there, not even discussion. The center of Negro intellectual life in that black-belt county was a small Negro college struggling for existence in the midst of what I had come to know as rural southern poverty. I have no present recollection of what I said to the overflow crowd in that little church that Sunday afternoon. I do have the feeling, however, that whatever I said must have fallen on deaf ears. The march from Selma to Montgomery to enforce the long recognized right of blacks to vote came a decade later.

When I returned to New York work had already begun on the new mandate. Up to this historical juncture we never really had to confront the harsh realities of a post-*Brown* era. We could no longer be ambivalent about the crucial question of whether we wanted the Court simply to order the immediate admission of the named petitioners or whether we wanted broader class relief. We had, of course, discussed these questions at great length, but the post-*Brown* era was now here. Previously in 1950, after four years of effort, we had succeeded in gaining the admission of a few black students to the Universities of Texas and Oklahoma on the graduate and professional school level.[3] This took place without disruption or violence, despite predictions to the contrary. But we and the nation had had no real experience with large scale desegregation efforts in the field of education.

In the 235-page brief on the first reargument of *Brown* in December 1953, in answer to questions 4 and 5, we had argued that the Fourteenth Amendment requires that a decree be entered directing that petitioners be admitted *forthwith* to public schools as the Court had ruled in the Texas and Oklahoma cases. In those cases the Court's rationale had been that constitutional rights are personal and present and therefore could not be postponed in the interest of permitting the state time to make necessary adjustments. Manifestly, those cases were distinguishable in an equity context. At the graduate and professional school level southern states had not set up a dual network of graduate and professional facilities for blacks. The number of blacks seeking advanced degrees was minimal. The out-of-state scholarship program, held unconstitutional in the *Gaines* case in 1938, had been devised to circumvent the state's obligation in this respect.[4] Citation of these graduate and professional school cases, therefore, did not help the court in its perplexing task.

Moreover, the Court must have found our "forthwith" argument ambiguous in view of the caption which preceded it in which we said: "After careful consideration of all of the factors involved in transition from segregated school *systems* to unsegregated school *systems,* appellants know of no reasons or considerations which would warrant postponement of the enforcement of appellants' rights by this Court in the exercise of its equity powers."[5] In other words, on the one hand, we talked of the "transition" from "segregated school systems" to "unsegregated school systems" in the caption and, on the other hand, we argued thereunder that the relief sought was the immediate admission of appellants. The immediate admission of appellants alone would not have resulted in the suggested transition. The dual school system would have remained intact.

Question no. 4 which the Court wanted answered again read as follows:
Assuming it is decided that segregation in public schools violates the Fourteenth Amendment
    (a) would a decree necessarily follow providing that, within the limits set by normal geographic school districting, Negro children should forthwith be admitted to schools of their choice, or
    (b) may this Court, in the exercise of its equity powers, permit an effective gradual adjustment to be brought about from existing segregated systems to a system not based on color distinctions?

This time in answer to question no. 4 we said, in essence, that the school authorities must still admit petitioners forthwith but could be given until September 1955 to complete "prerequisite administrative and mechanical procedures" necessary to admit "the complaining children and others similarly situated."[6] We did not emphasize normal geographic districting because even then we were haunted by the specter of housing segregation in the cities. We were essentially idealists. We had visions most of the time of a few black children scattered among many white pupils in each classroom, the way those of us who were reared in New England remembered it.

Question no. 5 which the Court wanted us to answer anew read:
On the assumption on which questions 4(a) and (b) are based, and assuming further that this Court will exercise its equity powers to the end described in question 4(b),
    (a) should this Court formulate detailed decrees in these cases;
    (b) if so what specific issues should the decrees reach;
    (c) should this Court appoint a special master to hear evidence with a view to recommending specific terms for

such decrees;

(d) should this Court remand to the Courts of first instance with directions to frame decrees in these cases, and if so, what general directions should the decrees of this Court include and what procedures should the courts of first instance follow in arriving at the specific terms of more detailed decrees?

In answer to question no. 5, we argued that if the Court should allow an "effective gradual adjustment" from segregated school systems to systems not based on color distinctions, it should not formulate detailed decrees but should remand the cases to the Courts of first instance with specific directions to complete desegregation by a day certain.[7] We also suggested an outside limit of September 1, 1956 in answer to question 5.[8] This would have set an outside limit of more than two years after the May 17, 1954 decision. We further urged that a decision granting the school authorities before the Court time "should be so framed that no other state maintaining such a system is lulled into a period of inaction and induced to merely await suit on the assumption that it will then be granted the same period of time after such suit is instituted."[9] Here we appeared to be reaching, in effect, for relief in suits not yet instituted, but the constitutional limitations of due process were readily apparent. What we really wanted was some statement from the Court to the effect that it hoped the rest of the south would accept its decision as the law of the land and avoid a multiplicity of similar suits.

Much to our surprise, on the second reargument in the Fall of 1954 the Court requested us to file still another brief solely on the class action aspect of these cases, i.e., the extent of the class and the effect of a decree on members of the class not before the Court. We, of course, argued that members of the class not before the Court were entitled to the same relief as the named petitioners. This additional brief was required because the respondent school authorities had argued that in so-called spurious federal class actions of the type brought in the *Brown* cases relief could be afforded only to those petitioners actually before the court. In so-called true class actions in the federal courts all members of the class were bound by the judgment and therefore entitled to relief whether present or not. This was a transparent attempt to limit the impact of *Brown* to the few remaining named petitioners. The cases had been pending so long that some of the petitioners had already finished school. We defined the class in that particular brief as all those attending and qualified to attend school in the particular school system before the court.[10] The Court agreed. On the surface this class relief argument again appeared inconsistent with our original forthwith stance as to the named petitioners, but this was not necessarily so. The Court could have ordered the named petitioners admitted forthwith and ordered unnamed members of the class admitted within the outer time limit of September 1956 which we had suggested. This would be Circuit Judge Potter Stewart's solution in 1956 in a similar case in Hillsboro, Ohio.[11] However, I cannot recall whether this was argued in the *Brown* case.

Although we vigorously denounced the policy of gradualism in the briefs we submitted, we privately feared that that path was inevitable as far as implementation of *Brown* was concerned. In September 1953, before the Court's '54 decision, the Topeka, Kansas School Board had adopted a resolution to the effect that its schools would be desegregated as rapidly as practicable. At the time of the second reargument, only fifteen percent of the 700 Negro elementary school children out of a total elementary school population of 8500 had been admitted to white schools in Topeka. There segregation had not even been compelled by the state; it was simply permitted in the elementary schools and only in city school districts. Topeka was at the opposite end of the spectrum with relation to communities like Clarendon County, South Carolina and Prince Edward County, Virginia where segregation was compulsory and black pupils greatly outnumbered white pupils in the public school population.

As noted, it was all too clear even in 1954 that there were severe limits to the judicial process. The courts were simply without power to enforce their decrees against determined official opposition. But we never dared to speak of the probable need for federal troops to enforce the Supreme Court's decision in answer to the south's prediction of massive resistance. Our hope after the second reargument was simply that the court would not formally substitute the philosophy of gradualism for the discarded doctrine of separate but equal. The phrase—"with all deliberate speed"—was indeed unfamiliar but, at the same time, its *déjà vu* quality was inescapable. It required no crystal ball to discern that gradualism had a new name and the South had a license for delay. As the Eighth Circuit Court of Appeals said a few years later:[12]

> It is, we think, quite generally recognized that a solution to the problem of effecting desegregation will in most instances have to come through a series of progressive, transitional steps. And the *Brown* decisions appear to permit of the handling of a situation in this manner, provided the school district engages in making a "reasonable start toward full compliance" and continues to move forward with "all deliberate speed."

That then unfamiliar phrase ushered in the era of tokenism. Pupil assignment and grade-a-year plans suggested by the federal government in its amicus curiae brief on the first reargument were devices by which tokenism was effected. Gradually, and with agonizing frustration, a few more black students were admitted to all-white schools. It soon became apparent that we would have to force a broader implementation of *Brown.*

We then became "disestablishmentarians".[13] We commenced framing complaints in school desegregation cases in which we requested in our prayers for relief the "disestablishment" of the dual school systems and the merging of these separate entities into a unitary system. We argued that *Brown* imposed on school officials operating dual school systems an affirmative duty to take action to merge the two systems; and that *Brown* was not simply a prohibition against denying a black student who might apply admission to a white school. This argument fell on some other deaf ears.

Urging that black teachers be assigned to white schools as a part of the teaching of *Brown* redefined our goals for a bewildered black community which still wondered what would happen to black schools. On the other hand, this broader approach probably increased resistance to *Brown* in those white communities which viewed black teachers as inferior.

Most southerners had undoubtedly come to believe in 1959, when we first advocated "disestablishmentarianism", that the worst result one could expect from the Supreme Court's decision was some blacks in school with whites. And the majority of the white population in the rest of the country probably hoped we would accept this new compromise of constitutional rights, especially after federal troops had to be sent into Little Rock to enforce the right of a few black children to enter the high school there.

This narrow view of the impact of *Brown* had also settled upon a large part of the black community which found the price of desegregation too high. For example, schools in Little Rock had been closed for a time; the University of Georgia had also been temporarily closed in a back-breaking effort to secure the admission of two students; all schools in Prince Edward County had been closed and remained closed for a decade; the best black teachers were being assigned to white schools; the best black students were being admitted to white colleges; and the best black pupils were being assigned under pupil assignment to white schools. This more restricted view of *Brown* thus became a major roadblock to wider implementation.

We lawyers had also accepted the fact that in the deep south the need for getting started was paramount. Desegregation had gone forward in the District of Columbia, Delaware, Kansas and some other border states, but everyone knew where the real problem was. We were so anxious to get on with the business of desegregation in the deep south by 1958 that we abandoned the

Clarendon County, South Carolina and Prince Edward County, Virginia suits, two of the original cases argued with *Brown,* until urban communities with predominantly white school populations had been desegregated. We did this because black pupils outnumbered white pupils by about 7-1 in those counties. A suit was filed in Atlanta pursuant to this strategy in 1958, followed by the filing or pushing of suits previously filed in other major southern cities.

Our best laid plans for speeding desegregation were derailed, however, not only by the unfamiliar phrase with which we had to deal but by the confluence of many other foreseen and unforeseen events. As blacks began marching to the beat of a different drummer, the south could not believe its ears. It retaliated with massive resistance to school desegregation as promised. We had been forewarned of massive resistance in the deep south, but we did not know when or where it would strike or what form it would take.

We did not realize, for example, that by pushing for desegregation on the college level in Alabama and by supporting the Montgomery bus boycott in 1956 we would bring on retaliatory action from state authorities which would have the effect of barring the NAACP from operating in Alabama for years. Alabama invoked its foreign corporations law and demanded the membership list. Other states instituted legislative investigations of the NAACP and the LDF.

Antiquated legal concepts such as barratry, champerty and maintenance were resurrected and reenacted into law in Virginia in an attempt to castrate the legal effort which culminated in the *Brown* decision and to prevent its implementation and expansion into other areas of the public life. These terms, aimed at controlling the conduct of lawyers as well as laymen, embodied prohibitions against stirring up litigation, financing of law suits, and "ambulance chasing".

Plaintiffs and prospective plaintiffs in school desegregation cases were visited with economic reprisals. Others were frightened off by the mere prospect of such reprisals. Negro teachers and principals, an important segment of the economic life line of the black communities, were threatened with retrenchment.

We had not anticipated that the black community in Montgomery, Alabama would spontaneously strike out on its own desegregation program in 1956 and spark the antisegregation revolution in the black community for which *Brown* had provided the momentum. We had anticipated bringing suits in the deep south after *Brown* to desegregate other public facilities but our sainted Rosa Parks "jumped the gun." The suit, filed in 1955, for admission of two Negro women to the University of Alabama, had been proceeding peacefully until then. Suddenly, massive resistance emerged with some more unfamiliar phrases—"nullification and interposition"—as well as threats of violence and official outbursts of defiance of the Courts.

The lack of strong support for the *Brown* decision on the part of the Executive Branch of the national government in 1954 and the years immediately thereafter not only fed ambivalence about the correctness of the decision, but also emboldened southern governors and state legislators. An avalanche of anti-*Brown* statutes had to be declared unconstitutional. Our case load was mounting. Big money was hard to come by.

The Internal Revenue Service was persuaded in 1956 that the NAACP should divest itself of the formidable tax exempt Legal Defense Fund lest that tax exemption be taken away. This was a highly sophisticated body blow to the organization and its legal arm, inflicted by the national government. It frightened the leadership, led to internal organizational strife which greatly weakened both organizations, wrecked all plans for building black and white community support and for an orderly, coordinated progression of school desegregation lawsuits and lawsuits in other areas.

As a separate entity, the NAACP later, but perhaps prematurely, as some have claimed, carried the fight to *de facto* segregated school systems in the north and pressed for an even broader construction of *Brown* which had not been argued in those cases by counsel for petitioners. *Brown* had concerned itself only with state-enforced segregation and not with segregation resulting from residential patterns. The problem was, however, if the NAACP had not responded to the demand for action in *de facto* segregated school situations in the north, some other organization would have done so. One of the things we had learned by 1965, when these northern school cases got under way, was that we lawyers could not control the course of history. Our role was simply to represent those who demanded action by the state. Moreover there were many school situations in the north resulting from school board action and the action of other public officials which were clearly within the contemplation of *Brown*.

The Freedom Riders ignited the flames of massive resistance in Mississippi. That official resistance collided head-on with our efforts to gain the admission of a single Negro to the University of Mississippi. Although we had been preparing the suit for months, when I walked into friendly Judge Mize's court room in the Federal District Court in Jackson a few days after the Freedom Riders had arrived, he remarked to me that we had picked the wrong time to file any such suit. He had remembered me from 1949 when Judge Robert L. Carter and I filed suit to equalize Negro teachers' salaries in Jackson. We were perhaps the first black lawyers Mississippi had seen in court since reconstruction. The admission of James Meredith to the University of Mississippi cost the federal government millions of dollars. When I received an invitation a year or so ago from black law students at the University to speak at the law school, although I could not go to see for myself how the university had changed, I had long since concluded that the price of Meredith's admission was right.

When the Freedom Riders and sit-inners moved to center stage in 1960, all school desegregation suits in the south were virtually abandoned by our small, overworked LDF staff to take on a new and equally difficult legal battle. *Plessy v. Ferguson*,[14] the case which upheld separate but equal railroad cars, had to be overruled. The *Civil Rights Cases of 1883*,[15] which held the Civil Rights Act of 1875 unconstitutional, had to be reargued. The 1875 Act had been designed to secure the rights of blacks in privately owned places of public accommodation. Injunctions against Martin Luther King from Albany, Georgia in 1962 to Selma, Alabama in 1965 had to be vacated. The hundreds of jailed Freedom Riders and sit-inners also had to be defended against local prosecutions.

Birmingham was awash with violence when our second suit to desegregate the University of Alabama was filed in 1963, the first having failed. A Federal District Court promptly ordered the admission of two students. George Wallace carried out his threat, made in connection with the pending Birmingham Public School desegregation suit, to stand in the school house door, when the two black students were escorted to the university by federal marshals. Bull Connor, Chief of Police in Birmingham, had already turned his water hose and his dogs on marching blacks. During the Birmingham campaign we LDF lawyers used to catch that 7:00 p.m. flight from Newark to Birmingham so often that the stewardess once said to us, "Y'all live in Birmingham or New York?"

When Medgar Evers was killed in Jackson that summer, I gave Mississippi up "for dead." I had been there 22 times on the University of Mississippi case alone and so I figured my nine lives had run out. I shall never forget that trip from Jackson to the Federal Court House in Meridian during the Meredith case. We were on our way to the Court House to file a contempt of court action against the Governor of Mississippi who had called for massive resistance on the part of every Mississippi official. Medgar was driving as he had done so often. I sat beside him in the front seat. My secretary and James Meredith sat in the back. When we came to a familiar stretch of road running through a deserted wooded area Medgar said, "Don't turn around now, but we are being followed by a state trooper." James Meredith's admission to the University of Mississippi cost the black community Medgar Evers's life.

By the time we got back to more than 100 pending school desegregation cases in 1965, the *Brown* decision was well on its way to being effectively overruled by the in-migration of blacks to the decaying central cities and the out-migration of whites to new suburban communities. When we filed suit to desegregate the public schools in Atlanta, Georgia, in 1958, for example, the school population was about forty percent black and sixty percent white. Today, the school population of Atlanta is about eighty percent black. Atlanta now has a black superintendent of schools and a black mayor. Thus, while everything else in the public life of Atlanta is desegregated twenty years after *Brown,* the schools are not. In New York City whites are now considered a minority in the school system.

In the deep south no school board came forward with a plan of its own to desegregate its schools. A law suit had to be brought in virtually every instance if any movement toward desegregation was to be expected. Most black parents remained fearful for the safety and emotional well being of their children and black teachers continued to see only job losses for their ranks. Relief from the impossible task of trying to carry a nation-wide load of school desegregation suits came for the hard pressed LDF lawyers in the form of congressional authorization for justice department sponsored school desegregation suits by the Civil Rights Act of 1964. Of course, executive action with respect to the bringing of lawsuits is wholly dependent on the domestic policy of the current administration but this monumental piece of legislation meant that the national congress had once again assumed its responsibility to enact legislation to enforce the Fourteenth Amendment.

The years have indeed gone by. It is now twenty years after the Supreme Court said segregation of Negro children in the public schools generates "A feeling of inferiority" in them "as to their status in the community that may affect their hearts and minds in a way unlikely ever to be undone." In the massive *de facto* segregated school systems in urban America today children of the "black is beautiful" era view pictures in their black studies classes of black members sitting on the Supreme Court, in the halls of Congress, in the President's cabinet, and at posts in all levels of federal, state and local government. The status of blacks in the national community since *Brown* has changed visibly. To the extent that opportunities for blacks to move into the mainstream increase, *Brown* is implemented. Moreover, television, which seems to have as much impact as elementary schools on the minds of young children, now portrays blacks as people who use the same toothpaste as their white counterparts, eat the same cereals, and buy the same patent medicines. It seems that today *Brown* has little practical relevance to central city blacks. Its psychological and legal relevance has already made an impact. Central city

20

blacks seem more concerned now with the political and economic power accruing from the new black concentrations than they do with busing to effect school desegregation. The dilemma for these blacks is real. It is diversified, but there is now a new national black community with pride in itself and its accomplishments.

In addition it appears that it may be meaningless to talk about feelings of inferiority to a black youth in the central city where blacks no longer consider themselves inferior to whites and no longer believe that any institution which is all white is necessarily good and ought to be integrated. *Brown* has been a second Emancipation Proclamation in that it has freed blacks from their own feelings of inferiority and absolved the white leadership class of its feelings of guilt. Thus, the rationale for *Brown* may have slipped away. It may need a new rationale that goes something like this: Segregation is bad because the only way blacks can get an equal education is to go where the money is.

We conceded in the *Brown* cases that the facilities provided black children were equal to those provided white children. We did this because we sought to eliminate any possibility for another decision based upon separate but equal. We wanted the Court to rule squarely on the issue of segregation itself. There had been enough cases like the Texas and Oklahoma cases based upon a finding that equal facilities had not been provided for blacks. We also had the feeling (as a result of this series of cases which began in 1936 with the admission of Donald Murray to the law school of the University of Maryland pursuant to an order of the highest court of that state)[16] that the time had come for black Americans to claim Charles Sumner's legacy.[17] Our concession has been construed, it seems, as a prohibition against looking anew at the physical equality issue in all black central city schools.

Consequently, for the future, it appears there are two very difficult legal problems ahead stemming from *Brown*. One is that posed by the quality of education afforded the black poor in segregated inner city schools. The other is that presented by the presence of a new black middle class seeking "reparations" when it comes to admission to higher educational facilities and to job opportunities in the school system's upper echelons.

In retrospect, it is difficult now to say whether desegregation of the public schools would have progressed more rapidly if the Supreme Court had adopted petitioners' view of the type of relief to which they were entitled and had never invoked the phrase "with all deliberate speed". What can be said with some certainty is that without *Brown* there would not have been a civil rights revolution.

¹⁻ *Brown v. Board of Education of Topeka,* 347 U.S. 483 (1954). The Court said:
"Because these are class actions, because of the wide applicability of this decision, and because of the great variety of local conditions, the formulation of decrees
in these cases presents problems of considerable complexity. On reargument, the
consideration of appropriate relief was necessarily subordinated to the primary
question—the constitutionality of segregation in public education. We have now
announced that such segregation is a denial of the equal protection of the laws. In
order that we may have the full assistance of the parties in formulating decrees, the
cases will be restored to the docket, and the parties are requested to present further
argument on Questions 4 and 5 previously propounded by the Court for the reargument this Term. The Attorney General of the United States is again invited to
participate. The Attorneys General of the states requiring or permitting segregation
in public education will also be permitted to appear as amici curiae upon request to
do so by September 15, 1954, and submission of briefs by October 1, 1954."

²⁻ *Brown v. Board of Education of Topeka,* 345 U.S. 972 (1953). The five questions
read as follows:
"Each of these cases is ordered restored to the docket and is assigned for
reargument on Monday, October 12, next. In their briefs and on oral argument
counsel are requested to discuss particularly the following questions insofar as they
are relevant to the respective cases:
1. What evidence is there that the Congress which submitted and the State
   legislatures and conventions which ratified the Fourteenth Amendment con-
   templated or did not contemplate, understood or did not understand, that it
   would abolish segregation in public schools?
2. If neither the Congress in submitting nor the States in ratifying the Fourteenth Amendment, understood that compliance with it would require the
   immediate abolition of segregation in public schools, was it nevertheless the
   understanding of the framers of the Amendment
   (a) that future Congresses might in the exercise of their power under sec-
       tion 5 of the Amendment, abolish such segregation, or
   (b) that it would be within the judicial power, in light of future conditions,
       to construe the Amendment as abolishing such segregation of its own
       force?
3. On the assumption that the answers to questions 2 (a) and (b) do not dispose
   of the issue, is it within the judicial power, in construing the Amendment, to
   abolish segregation in public schools?
4. Assuming it is decided that segregation in public schools violates the Fourteenth Amendment
   (a) would a decree necessarily follow providing that, within the limits set by
       normal geographic school districting, Negro children should forthwith
       be admitted to schools of their choice, or
   (b) may this Court, in the exercise of its equity powers, permit an effective
       gradual adjustment to be brought about from existing segregated sys-
       tems to a system not based on color distinctions?
5. On the assumption on which questions 4 (a) and (b) are based, and assuming
   further that this Court will exercise its equity powers to the end described in
   question 4 (b),
   (a) should this Court formulate detailed decrees in these cases;
   (b) if so what specific issues should the decrees reach;
   (c) should this Court appoint a special master to hear evidence with a view
       to recommending specific terms for such decrees;
   (d) should this Court remand to the courts of first instance with directions
       to frame decrees in these cases, and if so, what general directions should
       the decrees of this Court include and what procedures should the courts
       of first instance follow in arriving at the specific terms of more detailed
       decrees?
            The Attorney General of the United States is invited to take part in
       the oral argument and to file an additional brief if he so desires."

³⁻ *Sweatt v. Painter,* 339 U.S. 629 (1950); *McLaurin v. Oklahoma State Regents*

339 U.S. 637 (1950); *Sipuel v. Board of Regents*, 332 U.S. 631 (1948).

[4] *Missouri ex rel. Gaines v. Canada*, 305 U.S. 337 (1938).

[5] At page 190.

[6] At page 10.

[7] At page 24.

[8] At page 29.

[9] At page 2.

[10] At page 4.

[11] *Clemons v. Board of Education of Hillsboro*, 228 F.2d 853 (6th Cir.) *cert. den.* 350 U.S. 1006 (1956).

[12] *Dove v. Parham*, 282 F.2d 256, 259 (8th Cir. 1960).

[13] It appears that the first time a court used the word "disestablish" with reference to the requirements of Brown was in *Parham v. Dove*, 271 F.2d 132, 138 (8th Cir. 1959). There the court said:

> "The lack of any affirmative plan or action to disestablish the segregation status which had unconstitutionally been set up in the District, other than as the Board might be called upon to deal under the provisions of the 1956 or the 1959 Act with some individual application for assignment to another school, would perhaps not measure up to the legal and moral responsibility resting on a Board under the expression and holding of the *Brown* casses."

[14] 163 U.S. 537 (1896).

[15] 109 U.S. 3 (1883).

[16] *Pearson, et al. v. Murray*, 182 A. 590 (Ct. of Appeals, Md. 1936).

[17] Charles Sumner argued the case of *Roberts v. City of Boston*, 5 Cush. (Mass.) 198 (1849), in which he sought to secure the admission of black pupils in Boston's public school system to white schools long before the adoption of the Fourteenth Amendment. He was later a Massachusetts Senator and the leader in the Congress with respect to post-Civil War Amendments and civil rights legislation designed to enforce those amendments.

Delaware's Contribution to *Brown*

Louis L. Redding

I am somewhat embarrassed at being included in this panel which is composed almost entirely of experts in the broad field of civil rights and civil liberties, because I am not an expert in constitutional law nor am I an expert in that narrower division of constitutional law which might be called civil rights and civil liberties. I am just a pedestrian, journeyman lawyer who happens to have been practicing in a state where the necessities of the situation made me participate in civil rights activities.

But one does not have to be deeply versed in constitutional law to feel the kind of urge that black lawyers all over the United States sometimes feel which impels them into this kind of activity. I think that perhaps one of the leading exponents of involvement was a man who in my youth was certainly a mentor of mine through his writings, Dr. W. E. B. DuBois. When I was a child as NAACP members, we took in our home *The Crisis,* the organ of that organization, of which he was the editor. My parents bought his books, and I grew up on the kind of social philosophy that Dr. DuBois espoused. I remember among other things a description that he gave of the status of black people in this country, and he said (and he said this just about a year after *Plessey v. Ferguson*): "They do not share, speaking of black people, the full national life because there has always existed in America a conviction varying in intensity but always widespread that people of Negro blood should not be admitted into the group life of the nation, no matter what their condition might be."

So prevalent was this conviction of the propriety of the exclusion of blacks from normal participation in community life in the state in which I was admitted to the bar, that, at the time of my admission, racial discrimination had been challenged in the courts in only one case, that of *Neal v. Delaware.* In this case which went to the United States Supreme Court that court reversed the conviction of a Negro who had been sentenced to be hanged, and reversed that conviction on the grounds that Negroes had been excluded from the Grand Jury which indicted the defendant.

In many areas of community life in that state there were positive constitutional or statutory provisions imposing discrimination: in public education at all levels; in places of public accommodation, such as inns, restaurants, theatres, in public carriers. I should, I suppose, for the sake of accuracy, acknowledge that although legislation permitted segregation in public carriers it had never actually been practiced. Legislation commanded racial segregation in public and in private hospitals, and though they received public subsidy, they followed the practice of racial segregation. There was racial segregation in seating in courtrooms, and in those same courtrooms blacks were rarely, if ever, addressed by the normal terms of civil respect, "Mr." or "Mrs." It was also notorious that differential punishment (unfavorable to blacks) was meted out to whites convicted of crimes victimizing blacks, and to blacks convicted of offences against whites. There was segregation in jail. In employment, blacks were relegated to the physically most arduous and most unattractive work. And the appointment of a black to the most menial job in state or county or municipal government was a noteworthy event. As I look back upon that dreary picture of segregation in all aspects of community life, the only redeeming feature I can remember is that the so-called Public Library,—it was called a Public Library but it was privately endowed—was the one institution in all of community life that I can think of where there was never any sign of racial segregation. And that, I can assure you, was the one place where many black youths like myself, growing up in the community, spent much of their time.

Desegregating the University of Delaware

It was against this kind of community background twenty-five years ago that a score of students from what was originally called rather quaintly the "State College for Colored Students" sought to apply for admittance to the undergraduate college of the University of Delaware. They were denied application forms by the administrative staff so they simply wrote letters of application to the state university. All their applications were rejected. On their behalf I wrote a letter to the President of the Board of Trustees of the university. It detailed in four pages deficiencies at the black state-supported college, deficiencies the accrediting association had documented and as a result of which had denied accreditation to the black college. It was, of course, this lack of accreditation that had motivated this group of black youths to seek admission to the state university. My letter, addressed to the President of the Board of Trustees, asked that he call a special meeting of the Board of Trustees to act upon these requests for admittance. After a few days, I received his reply to my four-page letter—four lines typed on the letterhead of the law firm that he had established after a ten-year stint as a federal judge. (He was able to retire with full salary and reap the benefit of the kind of corporate practice that Delaware affords a great many lawyers.) Well, this President of the Board of Trustees sent me this four-line letter in which he indicated that in his own good time he would call a special meeting of the Board of Trustees. So I wrote back and said in effect, "Look, Sir, I didn't write to you in your capacity as a private citizen; I wrote to you as President of the Board of Trustees of the state university, a state agency, and will you please respond to my letter as the president of a state agency should respond?" He did send another letter, quite promptly, in which he stated that he was calling a special meeting of the Board of Trustees of the university to act upon these applications.

It would be a very interesting thing if you knew the state, or if I could give you the picture of the kind of people who made up the Board of Trustees. The composition of the Board of Trustees of the state university of course was provided for by state law: a certain number were appointed by the Governor, there were certain ex officio members, such as the Superintendent of the State Department of Public Instruction, and the President of the university. These members then appointed other members of the board, and of course the other members were usually the very wealthy. Perhaps you know the name "duPont". There were about four members of the duPont family on the board; the Chancellor of our State Court of Chancery was a member of the board; the Chief Justice of the State Supreme Court was a member of the board. Well, they held their special meeting, and I got a letter from them which said something like this: ". . . Because the applicants do not come within the description of applicants to this university as provided in a certain resolution of the Board of Trustees, they are denied admission to the university."

Almost immediately we filed an action in our Court of Chancery, and Delaware may be the last remaining state which has a separate court of equity, presided over by a judge called "Chancellor." This action that we filed, prior to the decision in *Brown v. Board of Education,* was based on two legal theories, the first that racial segregation in and of itself violated the equal protection clause of the Fourteenth Amendment. And we fell back on an alternative theory, in the event racial segregation was not held violative of the Constitution. The alternative theory was that the facilities at the black college were inferior in quality to the facilities of the state university. Among other approaches, we used a number of experts in an attempt to establish that the facilities at the black colleges were inferior to those of the state university. After a somewhat lengthy trial, requiring a week or more, the Chancellor rendered a decision. He stated that, considering prior decisions of the United States Supreme Court—he could not declare segregation in and of itself violative of the Constitution. However, he decided in favor of the black applicants on the narrow ground that the facilities were unequal; and ordered the immediate admission of the young people who had applied for admission. That decision was rendered in August, 1950.

Soon after events in the state caused the filing of two other cases in the Court of Chancery, and these cases became part of the case decided on May 17, 1954, *Brown v. Board of Education of Topeka.*

School Cases in Delaware

In a small rural community called Hockessin, Delaware, where the Delaware hills begin to verge into southeastern Pennsylvania, an elderly couple had adopted a little girl. On wintry mornings the mother watched as a school bus passed her home transporting white children to the "white" elementary school in the village. There was no bus to carry black children to the "colored" school although en route to the "white" school the bus with white pupils did pass the "colored" school. One morning the elderly mother approached the bus driver and requested him to stop for her six-year old daughter and to leave her at the "colored" school, which he passed on the way to the "white" school. The "colored" school was about two miles from the home of this child. The bus driver told the mother that his bus was for white children and therefore he could not carry her child. Successively the mother wrote to the school principal, to the State Superintendent of Education, and to the governor of the state. But all replied, in substance, that the bus was for pupils at the white school and not for pupils attending the black school.

Finally the mother came to Wilmington to talk to a lawyer, and she showed him copies of her letters seeking to get her child on the bus and the replies. What the mother indicated to the lawyer was that she wanted her daughter to ride to the "colored" school on the school bus because she believed that some part of the taxes that she and her husband paid contributed to the purchase of that school bus.

What the lawyer told the mother was that he would not be interested in trying to get her child on that bus merely to ride to the "colored" school, but that if she were interested in having her child ride the school bus with the white children to attend the school to which they went, he would undertake to see if that could be accomplished. Well, it was a marvellous thing to watch—it was a wonderful thing to watch this mother's amazement at the proposal that she attempt, through a lawsuit, to get her child into the segregated "white" school. And finally she agreed.

About the same time, in another community in Delaware, parents of pupils of high school age had become concerned that their children could not go to the high school in the community in which they lived but had to take public transportation into the city of Wilmington which was about eight miles away, to go to the only black high school maintained in the county. They went to the same lawyer; and simultaneoulsy these two suits were filed, one to gain admittance to the "white" elementary school, and one to gain admittance to the "white" high school.

Again, as in the college case, we sought to have the Chancellor declare segregation, in and of itself, violative of the equal protection clause of the Fourteenth Amendment. Again, however, the Chancellor said he was powerless to do so because precedents of the United States Supreme Court precluded him from so deciding. However, he did declare that he believed the separate-but-equal doctrine should be rejected and that such rejection must come from the highest court in the land.

Two years after the Chancellor's decision of April 1, 1952, these Delaware school cases which I have described, with similar cases from Kansas, South Carolina and Virginia and a separate case from the District of Columbia, were decided by the Supreme Court in the historic event which we mark today.

Speeding Reforms

Joseph B. Robison

I am taking the liberty of going back a little bit beyond *Brown* to begin my remarks today, to an event that took place just about the time that I started to work for the American Jewish Congress in 1946. During that year there had been a new wave of lynchings in the south and the government, under President Truman, responded, as the government so often responds, by appointing a commission. Called the President's Committee on Civil Rights, it was headed by an industrialist, Charles E. Wilson, President of the General Electric Company. Nobody expected anything to come of it.

The committee deliberated for nearly a year and a half and finally came out with its report, entitled, "To Secure These Rights." It was really a shocker and signalled a significant change in the nature of the civil rights movement in this country.

Everybody had expected the committee to come out for propaganda and for brotherhood and so forth. Instead, its report condemned segregation without reservation and demanded legislation; in short, really sweeping changes in the whole approach to civil rights. It was the sort of thing that the civil rights organizations, which then were a very small group, had been demanding all along.

Unfortunately, the report met the fate that government commission reports usually meet. In fact, I think there is a very interesting phenomenon that operates generally with respect to commissions. They are almost always more liberal than the community as a whole. No matter how they are constituted, no matter what kind of balancing of conservative and liberal forces is attempted, they virtually always come out with a liberal report. This is because when they really look at the facts, they find that that is what is really required. Unfortunately, the report is usually too liberal for the country to adopt. For example, the drug abuse commission came out with a demand for vast changes in the laws on that subject; yet its proposals have been pretty well ignored in the years since.

Similarly, the recommendations of the President's Civil Rights Committee were not adopted for years. Ultimately almost all of them were adopted. As a matter of fact, one of the most significant was the recommendation that there be a permanent Civil Rights Commission in the United States government, and your president and the chairman of this meeting, Father Hesburgh, served with distinction on that commission. The segregation laws have been condemned. There is a fair employment practices law; there is a fair education practices law; and there is even a fair housing law, a national fair housing law, which the President's Committee did not dare to recommend. That was just a little bit too much for them.

But following the pattern of commission recommendations generally, these reforms were achieved ten, fifteen, or twenty years after they were formulated, with the result that the problems to which they were addressed had drastically changed by the time the reforms went into effect, and instead of those reforms we needed others.

I suggest that this is a reflection of a problem in our society, a problem with which lawyers and organized civic groups have to deal more effectively than they have in the past. I refer to the general stodginess of our democratic system. It always takes ten or fifteen years to put into effect the reforms that we recognize as necessary. (As Judge Motley has just shown, it has taken years to put into effect even the reforms required by the Supreme Court decision in the *Brown* case.) The result is that, by the time the reforms go into effect, the problems are different and we no longer face the situation for which the reforms were designed.

Title VI

For example, one of the most important recommendations of the president's committee was Title VI. They did not call it Title VI, but that is what it is called now. I refer to Title VI of the Civil Rights Act of 1964, which bars discrimination in any operation financed by the government. This provision embodies a really obvious principle, a principle that should have been assumed all along under our constitutional system. Is it not clear that, since the Constitution bars discrimination by government agencies, any agency that gets money from the government may not discriminate?

The president's committee recommended in 1948 that this principle be enforced by statute. But it was not until 1964 that its recommendation was finally put into effect. It has been moderately effective. However, by 1964, the operations financed by the federal government, and financed in a highly discriminatory fashion, had become so extensive that discrimination had become a deeply entrenched part of our system and extremely difficult to eradicate.

Perhaps the most significant example of this is in the field of housing—and your chairman was kind enough to mention that I have been involved in that to some extent.

The first bills proposing fair housing legislation anywhere in the country were introduced in the New York State Legislature in 1948. The first significant one to be adopted was in New York City in 1956. The federal law was not adopted until 1968. But 1948 was the critical time. This was the period immediately after World War II when the whole nature of the housing operations in this country was being vastly changed. They were being recast largely by a man named William Levitt who was creating monster housing developments, starting with Levittown, N.Y. His example was being followed all over the country.

If, at this critical time, Levitt and others creating that kind of housing development had been persuaded by argument or compelled by law to adopt the principle of nondiscrimination, the whole nature of our society would have been changed. We would not have had the white suburban nooses around our cities with the black cores in the center. Then we would have had a society in which *Brown* could have been more effective, in which all the reforms recommended by the President's Committee could have been more effective.

Unfortunately, we did not have the forces to persuade nor did we have the law to compel. Levitt adopted the "whites only" policy which had long been the general rule in the housing industry and all the other monster developments that were created about the same time followed suit. By the time we got the fair housing laws into effect, the white noose was already there. Getting black families into these large white developments became extremely difficult. They did not want to go, for obvious reasons. Hence, the pattern has more or less stayed the same despite the adoption of fair housing laws in a number of states prior to 1968 and, finally, the adoption of a federal law in that year.

This is not a phenomenon limited to civil rights. For example, the decisions of the Supreme Court condemning legislative malapportionment came too late to save the cities. For years and years, the cities were under-represented in Congress and in the state legislatures due to outrageous malapportionment. The Supreme Court finally got around to condemning that practice but by that time there had been a massive shift to the suburbs and legislative reapportionment benefited the suburbs rather than the cities.

Certainly, the problem is still with us. Consider the 1968 Report of the Kerner Commission, a sort of modern-day version of the Civil Rights Committee Report twenty years earlier. This was the commission that was established under the chairmanship of former Governor Otto Kerner of Illinois after the riots in 1967 and 1968. It came out with a marvelous set of recommendations, 81 of them, starting off with the necessity of reordering our priorities and spending less on the military budget and more on domestic affairs. Very fine recommendations. Very few of them have been adopted. They may be adopted in the 80s—but they were designed to cure the problems of the 60s not those of the 80s.

The Effects of *Brown*

I am not by any means saying that the *Brown* decision was useless or that it had no impact; it was absolutely vital to all future progress. To begin with, there is no doubt that it pulled out the stopper on federal legislation. There had been no civil rights laws passed by the United States Congress since the reconstruction period. The *Brown* decision came in 1954. The first twentieth century civil rights act came in 1957. There was another in 1960, and then the very broad ones of 1964 and 1968. These laws have certainly increased the participation of blacks north and south in all aspects of our lives, and vastly increased Negro voting in the south and public office holding as well.

As one who is closely involved, I find that one of the most striking changes that took place after *Brown* was a sharp rise in the level of public awareness of the civil rights issue. Prior to 1954, anybody involved in this activity had to sweat blood to get a story two inches long on the back pages of a newspaper. Maybe a lynching might make the front page; maybe the president's committee's report might be on the front page for a day or so. But there was relatively little coverage of race relations in this country, in the newspapers, in the magazines, and on the air. Since May 1954 there has been a tremendous flood of material on civil rights. The issue is never off the front pages of our newspapers for long. It figures one way or another in virtually every presidential election and in most congressional elections. It arises in some form or other in almost every session of Congress.

A totally different level of understanding has developed. Few question now that we have a race problem or that there is still a vast amount of inequality. And there is at least some understanding of the fact that we have to do something about it, although there is still serious resistance in the area of action.

I agree with Judge Motley that the decision of the Supreme Court in 1955 to apply its 1954 anti-segregation ruling on a gradual basis was a disaster. We cannot really know what would have happened if the Court had said, "Do it now." Undoubtedly, there would have been an awful row but my recollection of the period was that, in the months immediately following the 1954 decision, the white south was in a state of shock. Up to that time, it had been taken for granted that, when the Supreme Court issued a decision, you complied with it—and they were prepared to comply with it. There would have been resistance. But it would not have been organized in the way it was after the 1955 ruling, which gave the southern governments a chance to reorganize and grid themselves for total war. It was a very serious mistake. I think that it was done with good will but it was a disaster.

The topic this morning is *The Brown Decision: Reflections on the Continuing Challenge.* In view of the fact that this meeting is being held at a law school, the speakers are all lawyers, and most of the audience are lawyers or law students, I presume that we are concerned primarily with the continuing challenge to us as lawyers.

No doubt, we will want to pat ourselves on the back for what has been accomplished in the courts and in the legislatures. I question, however, whether the legal profession as a whole is entitled to do that. We have to recognize that it was the lawyers who put segregation into the statute books in the first place and it was they who put the segregation decisions into the law reports.

I am reminded of a piece by the well-known humorist, Frank Sullivan, parodying the typical radio family program. He presented "The Jukes Family," a "not-quite-bright family of the lower lower class." At one point, he has Ma Jukes complaining that the farmer down the road resented (with a gun) their borrowing a few chickens "after the way we all pitched in an' helped, the night his barn took fire." Pa responds that "we wa'n't doin' mor'n our plain duty in helpin' put that fire out. You know's well's I do, 'twas our Buster set that barn afire," Buster, of course, being the firebug of the family. How proud can we be as lawyers for what has been done for equality in view of the fact that we have really been undoing our own bad work?

Of course, the job ahead is not one for lawyers alone. We consistently solve our problems too late largely because we do not get enough guns to bear on our targets. When the democratic system was originally adopted back in the eighteenth century, it was the majority of the people who needed it. It was the majority of the people who were poor. It was the majority who were underprivileged, and were discriminated against by the legal system. Hence, it was a neat and effective concept that, if you gave the people power to vote and to control the government, the majority would cure their ills pretty fast. By and large, they did.

The trouble is that, today, the poor and underprivileged are a minority, not only in the racial sense but also in the sense that the poor people do not constitute an effective working majority. Today, the majority of people are relatively comfortable. They may be prepared to accept the fact that there is inequality, that there is poverty, and that something should be done about it. But there is no way of solving any of these problems that is not going to hurt the majority to some extent. They will have to make some sacrifice. The sacrifice may be only in the form of higher taxes, and this they view as bad enough. But usually something more is demanded.

My experience tells me that the majority is not likely to sacrifice readily. Hence, if reforms depend on majority consent—as they do under our system— we are not going to be able to achieve them unless we persuade the majority that they are going to be a lot more uncomfortable if the reforms are not made. In other words, we will have to persuade the majority, if only by raising hell, that whatever price they have to pay is worth the candle.

This is going to mean a good deal more than legal activity. The legal techniques are there and the lawyers are there. What we need is more in the way of organization, in the way of hell-raising by every legitimate form of protest. If we achieve that, and there have been signs that it may be achieved, we can close the destructive time lapse between understanding what society has to do and getting it done.

Segregation Based on Language

José A. Cabranes

The discussion of *Brown v. Board of Education* at this conference has left few aspects of that decision unexamined. But our work here would not be complete if we adjourned without considering another pernicious form of discrimination in education that flourishes in our schools today virtually untouched by the decision in *Brown*.

In *Brown*, the Supreme Court assumed the possibility that black schools could be equal to those provided for white children with respect to physical plant, curriculum, faculty and other tangible factors. The Court condemned the segregation of the facilities not because they were different, but because to separate children "of similar age and qualifications solely because of their race generates a feeling of inferiority as to their status in the community that may affect their hearts and minds in a way unlikely ever to be undone." In fashioning its decision, the Court reviewed social science materials indicating the nature and extent of the detrimental impact of separate education on black children.

Racial segregation, the Court found, could instill a sense of inferiority in black people that could affect its victims' social and economic relationships throughout their lives.

The poisonous experience of segregation in our schools continues despite *Brown*. School segregation affects not only our various black communities. It also distorts the lives of thousands of Puerto Ricans, Chinese Americans, Mexican Americans and other minority group children who may attend schools which are not only equal, but possibly the very same facilities attended by white children. Nevertheless, they are systematically separated from the educational opportunities provided all other students.

This widespread process of segregation and human deterioration is not based on intelligence or capability to learn or even on race alone. It is based primarily on an inability to understand the language of instruction.

Language Segregation

Language segregation exists wherever a substantial number of children who know little or no English must attend public schools without the benefit of adequate remedial programs in language skills.

Who are the non-English-speaking people of the United States at the present time? Almost all are Chinese, Puerto Rican, Mexican American, Filipino or native American. All of the groups currently suffering language segregation are groups which may also be defined in terms of race and/or national origin. Segregation based on language is rooted in racial or ethnic discrimination but it is a form of segregation one degree removed from purely racial discrimination.

In considering the effects of linguistic discrimination, we might do well to recall the approach of the Supreme Court in *Brown*. As the Court examined the consequences of racial discrimination on black children in *Brown*, we might explore the economic and social conditions of those who now suffer from discriminatory practices related in substantial measure to language.

Puerto Ricans form one of the largest groups of people victimized by such practices and the one with which I am most familiar. There are approximately two million Puerto Ricans in the continental United States. As a group, Puerto Ricans are the most severely deprived Americans in the cities of this nation.

For example, the 1970 census indicates that the median number of years of schooling for New York City's one million Puerto Ricans was eight and one half grades—more than two full grades below the level of the local black population. Of all Puerto Rican adults over twenty-five only forty-four percent had received more than an eighth grade education (compared to 66.8 percent for New York City's black population). A mere twenty percent had graduated from high school (compared to forty-one percent for New York City's black population). Only one Puerto Rican in one hundred had a college degree. One significant index of the Puerto Rican condition today is the incredible situation in the legal profession of New York. Fewer than seventy out of more than one million Puerto Ricans are admitted to the practice of law.

No one will be surprised by the correlated social and economic condition of Puerto Rican communities in the continental United States. The census found that more than 300,000 of New York City's one million Puerto Ricans—fully 35.1 percent of New York's Puerto Rican community—lived below the poverty line. Between 1960 and 1970, when median family income among whites in New York City rose twenty-six percent (from $6,365 to $10,378) and twenty-four percent among blacks (from $4,437 to $7,150), family income among Puerto Ricans rose by only thirteen percent (from $3,811 to $5,575).

The census to which I have just made reference reveals the pattern by which linguistic discrimination operates relentlessly to drive a specific class of people out of the public school system and, consequently, out of the social and economic mainstream of American life. Just as separate schools in *Brown* fastened a badge of inferiority on black people and denied them the equal protection of the laws, so the separation and isolation resulting from inadequate skills in English deny the children of Puerto Ricans and other minorities equal educational opportunities from the first day they enter a classroom.

Federal Law and Language Segregation

The problems facing millions of children of limited English-speaking ability were first recognized on a national level by the United States Congress in the Voting Rights Act of 1965. Section 4(e) of that statute invalidated state English literacy tests with respect to anyone who completed the sixth grade in an "American-Flag" school where the classroom language was other than English. This provision was upheld by the Supreme Court, which noted that it "may be viewed as a measure to secure for the Puerto Rican community residing in New York non-discriminatory treatment by government— both in the imposition of voting qualifications and the provision or administration of governmental services, such as public schools, public housing and law enforcement."

In 1968, Congress for a second time took notice of the phenomenon of language segregation. In that year it approved the Bilingual Education Act (20 U.S.C. §880(b) *et seq.*), which provides funds to local educational agencies for "new and imaginative elementary and secondary school programs designed to meet these special educational needs." In the 1974 fiscal year, $59,800,000 is available for this purpose.

These federal laws are in the nature of affirmative action programs. Both laws recognize that inaction and exclusion are the inevitable effect—and usually the intended effect—of laws and policies which seem to be neutral in character. The fact is that we can readily identify the victims of legislation which mandates the use of English only in our educational and governmental processes: namely, Oriental Americans, Mexican Americans, native Americans and, most recently, Puerto Ricans.

The Supreme Court and Language Segregation

The Supreme Court recently focused its attention on the problem of linguistic neutrality in *Lau v. Nichols,* a case involving public school students of Chinese ancestry. According to a report submitted to the Court, as of April 1973 there were 3,457 Chinese students in the San Francisco school system who spoke little or no English. About half of these students were receiving no special instruction to enable them to develop proficiency in the English language.

After observing that basic English skills are at the very core of a public school education, Mr. Justice Douglas stated for the majority, that "imposition of a requirement that, before a child can effectively participate in the educational program, he must already have acquired those basic skills is to make a mockery of public education."

The Court found it unnecessary to reach the question of whether the inaction of the San Francisco Public School System in *Lau* violated the Constitution. The Court did not rely on the equal protection clause of the Fourteenth Amendment. Instead, the Court relied solely on §601 of the Civil Rights Act of 1964, which bans discrimination based "on the ground of race, color, or national origin" in "any program or activity receiving federal financial assistance."

In contracting with the Department of Health, Education and Welfare for financial support, the defendant school district had agreed to comply with the Civil Rights Act and all requirements imposed by HEW pursuant to its regulation. Finding in favor of the plaintiff students, the Court cited the following guidelines, promulgated by HEW in 1970:

> Where inability to speak and understand the English language excludes national origin-minority group children from effective participation in the educational program offered by a school district, the district must take affirmative steps to rectify the language deficiency in order to open its instructional program to these students.

No remedy was proposed by the petitioners in *Lau.* The petitioners and *amici* had asked only "that the board of education be directed to apply its expertise to the problem and rectify the situation." The Court stated that teaching English to the plaintiffs, or providing courses of instruction in the Chinese language, were two approaches which might prove satisfactory.

"There may be others," the Court noted. Accordingly, the case was remanded to the Court below for the fashioning of appropriate relief.

Lau should not be read as a "Fourteenth Amendment Case" except in the derivative sense that the Court applied a statute which was firmly grounded on the Fourteenth Amendment. Moreover, the Court did not require "bilingual-bicultural" education, as some proponents of this program seem to believe. However, the Court did make a reference to bilingual education as one of the possible alternative courses of action available to the public school system. On the other hand, the Court's interpretation of the Civil Rights Act of 1964 and relevant administrative regulations presumably would be satisfied by a scheme merely to teach students the English language. What the Court did decide in *Lau*—at most—was this: that a public school is not free to ignore the language problems of any substantial number of its students. It cannot leave the problem entirely in the hands of the pupil and his parents by declaring that it provides the same facilities, textbooks, teachers and curriculum to all students. The Court effectively established the obligation of the public school to act—to do *something.*

Although the Court in *Lau* has assigned responsibility for language training to the public school system, nothing in its opinion precludes the participation of affected citizens in the shaping of educational programs designed to accomplish the statutory goal of equality of educational opportunity. In my view, bilingual-bicultural programs are most likely to flourish in communities where linguistic minorities constitute a substantial part of the total population and where citizen participation in the making of educational policy is well established.

By leaving the question of remedy to the lower courts, the Supreme Court has for the time being left open the issue of *which* program or programs would meet the objective of affording equality of educational opportunity for all students. That question—namely, the kind of program or programs which meet the statutory and constitutional goals of equal educational opportunity—is already before the lower federal courts in *Lau* itself and in another important language lawsuit brought in New York City.

Aspira's Case

In September, 1972, while I was serving as chairman of Aspira of New York, the Puerto Rican educational and leadership development agency, the organization filed suit in *Aspira of New York v. Board of Education of the City of New York.* Our counsel, the newly-formed Puerto Rican Legal Defense and Education Fund, presented arguments similar to those raised in *Lau.* Plaintiffs in the *Aspira* case allege that as many as 55,000 Spanish-speaking children in the federally assisted New York City School System are receiving no special training whatsoever in dealing with their English-language disability. Proceedings in the case were held in abeyance after the Supreme Court granted *certiorari* in *Lau.* However, on the basis of the *Lau* decision, plaintiffs have since moved for summary judgment. New developments should be forthcoming in the immediate future as the district court considers Aspira's argument that only a bilingual education program would meet the relevant tests in a city in which twenty-eight percent of the city's school children are of Hispanic origin.

For the Future

What is the meaning of all of this for the public school systems of those cities with substantial linguistic minorities? To state the matter in its simplest terms: the public schools must now recognize that the law will no more tolerate exclusionary policies based on language than it will tolerate exclusionary policies based on race. The public schools now are clearly on notice that it is their ultimate responsibility to teach basic skills in English usage to all their students in order to end language segregation.

However, in one important respect *Lau* differs from *Brown* and its progeny: it recognizes a need to treat some students differently from the larger mass of students. The net effect of requiring some form of special program for linguistic minority children is to sanction short-term segregation of students—at least long enough to derive the benefits of the special language program. But the long-range goal of *Lau* is entirely consistent with the *Brown* line of decisions: the elimination of language segregation altogether and the integration of linguistic minority groups into American society.

We know that the *Brown* decision, handed down twenty years ago, has not been fully implemented. Nevertheless, we know that significant progress has been made by black people in the intervening two decades. And we fully appreciate that the ethnic and linguistic minorities of the nation have benefitted greatly from the advances made possible by the black civil rights movement and the *Brown* decision. While traveling somewhat different routes, we continue to share a common interest in the achievement through law of equal educational opportunity for all our people.

The Post-*Brown* Decades

Richard G. Hatcher

In 1954, the Supreme Court drafted an obituary for segregation in education. Today, twenty years later, segregated education is alive and thriving throughout the land.

For two decades now, this country has been grappling with the landmark *Brown* decision. During these years, we have learned some bitter truths about ourselves.

We have found that America is gripped by forces promoting segregation in our schools, in our neighborhoods, and in all facets of our daily life.

We have found that to implement *Brown* we need at the least a quiet revolution in social and economic relationships—a revolution sapped before it begins by prevailing separatist notions among the people and by desperate "business as usual" sentiments on the part of our leadership.

We have also found that segregationists are committed to their separate schools with a passion worthy of Othello, with a cunning reminiscent of Iago and with a shrillness suitable to Desdemona, as played by a junior high school beauty queen.

Certainly, there has been some progress in the twenty years since *Brown.* But a national mandate to integrate our schools has not emerged.

Certainly, there are now black faces in formerly all white places. But, opponents of integration are quickly abandoning their violated temples of education, and heading for the hills—and the suburbs.

Certainly, barriers have fallen. But new barriers like educational tracking, and teacher testing, are rising to fill every breach in the segregationist ranks.

Let's take a look at the world of education today. Throughout Dixie, private schools created to counter integration are on the rise. In eight of eleven southern states, private school enrollment jumped forty-one percent from 1968 to 1972. For those students unwelcome at the new all-white academies, public schooling is the only option. And sometimes even that is not available. Prince Edward County in Virginia, apparently thrilled with the results of its private school experiment, closed its public schooling system for several years. Only recently, have the public schools reopened.

Gerrymandered school districts, carved to create racial enclaves, are now in vogue in the south. In Indianola, Mississippi, in Clarksdale, Mississippi, and elsewhere, specially constructed districts now keep white children and black children in their separate worlds during the school day. Redistricting in Roanoke Rapids, North Carolina has created a city school system that is ninety-seven percent white, while pushing black children out into a county system that is now heavily black.

Black children who can't be screened out by carefully-sculpted boundary lines are being pushed out of their schools—expelled and suspended—at an alarming rate. According to some estimates, up to 150,000 southern black students, mainly high school seniors, are being given the gate each year before they graduate. In Louisiana, some school districts have expelled as many as sixteen percent of the black student population. Even in northern cities, student pushouts are a problem. In Omaha, Nebraska, during the school year 1970-71, 1,095 black high school students—eight percent of the black student population—were expelled. During the same year, only 2.1 percent of the white student population was similarly disciplined.

Certainly, there are disciplinary problems in the schools. And today school administrators are solving these problems by pushing troubled students pell-mell into a world where they can become either misfits or menials or both.

In the north, since World War II, many larger cities have been Harlem-ized. Suburban homesteaders, nervously venturing into the metropolis during the day, sequester their families in distant villages, thereby doing their part to prevent "mongrelization" of the kindergartens.

In Gary, Indiana, a white exodus has helped produce a city of largely segregated schools. Some years ago, before I took office, Gary had a workable busing program that produced desegregated schools. But because Gary was a blue collar town the city authorities called the transportation shift a "school housing utilization program."

The people who worked in the city's steel mills appreciated the need for tight budgets, so the program ran into very little opposition. Today, due to demographic shifts, large-scale busing within the city limits is no longer a viable approach to schooling. And, beyond those city limits is a hostile and frightened northern Indiana population that would sooner let its children learn the three R's in a leper colony than permit busing between the Lake County countryside and downtown Gary schools.

Throughout the country, north and south, tracking and testing are currently in vogue among the neo-isolationists. Ghetto kids, often products of broken homes, always products of poor homes, are branded "inferior" early on and prepared for their roles as society's *Untermenschen*. Simultaneously, children from stable, middle-class homes are placed on the college preparatory "track."

The National Education Association, in a recent study, found that half of all schools in the south which were desegregating were simultaneously adopting tracking systems they had never used before.

These days after students are tested, separating the black chaff from the white grain, teachers are also tested to accomplish much the same thing. In 1972 the National Teacher's Examination (NTE), published by the Educational Testing Service, was required in 1,656 school districts in 11 southern states—and in only 52 northern and western school districts. Many thousands of black teachers have lost their jobs thanks to this experiment in racial quality control.

The NTE has recently been labeled discriminatory by a staff member of the Educational Testing Service. Its capacity to measure teaching ability is, certainly, questionable. Nonetheless, Mississippi, North Carolina and South Carolina now require a passing score on this test for all teachers in their states.

This NTE and other hurdles help to explain why black teachers in the south over the past twenty years have become an endangered species. Since 1954, the south has lost between 5,000 and 10,000 black teachers. Had there been no *Brown* decision, had separate but equal facilities and faculties been maintained, many thousands of black teachers would now have jobs in southern school systems—jobs held by white teachers today.

Even in those school systems where black teachers are hired, their presence often tends to be an anomaly. There are 22.5 pupils for each teacher in the United States. That's the national average. Let's take a look at black pupil/black teacher ratios on the high school level in larger cities in America. In each of these cities, there is a sizable black student population.

In Cincinnati, there are forty-eight black children for every single black teacher. In Columbus, Ohio, the ratio is fifty-one to one. The pupil/teacher ratio is fifty-three to one in Oakland, California; fifty-eight to one in Pittsburgh; sixty-two to one in San Francisco; seventy-nine to one in Buffalo;

eighty-three to one in New York City; and eighty-nine to one in Boston.

Eighty-nine to one. Aren't those incredible odds? Incredible odds against black children finding black models for their behavior? Incredible odds against black children finding teachers who know in their bones what it's like to be black in America, and who can deal with the provocative ways black kids sometimes cope with that painful fact.

In Gary, the black pupil teacher ratio is twenty-nine to one. Our school superintendent, who is white, has found that black teachers are available, anxious to teach in the inner cities, and effective in their pedagogical roles.

The *Brown* decision has not produced an overhaul in the American educational system, because it has not produced a revolution in American attitudes. Unquestionably, there have been major positive changes on all school levels. "Open admissions" policies at colleges, for instance, are now beginning to prove themselves out. At the City University of New York, some seven to ten students admitted in 1970 under the open door policy were still students two years later. The retention rate fails to support those educators who predicted massive drop-outs. It reinforces the simple but troublesome notion that black and other minority children want to get advanced schooling, and will work industriously and well if they are given the opportunity.

The new segregationists—the parents who send their children to all white academies; the teachers who seek security in separate and unequal schools; the blacks who fight busing to achieve integregation—are powerful today. Their efforts threaten the small advances made in the twenty years since *Brown.* Unless we are vigilant and resourceful, this country will produce from its educational institutions future student generations with baccalaureates in bitterness and doctorates in perpetual racial strife.

The Emerging Meanings
of Equal Educational Opportunities

David L. Kirp

Twenty years ago, when the *Brown* case was decided, the meaning of equal educational opportunity was relatively clear. The phrase was synonomous with an end to racial discrimination, an elimination of artificial barriers that separated blacks from whites. In the interval, the meaning of racial discrimination has changed, and those changes have produced a host of conflicts between historic allies. Equal educational opportunity has also acquired a host of new and broader non-racial meanings.

With respect to the racial issue three forces are pushing in quite different directions. First, black separatists, whose voice began to be heard in the late sixties, reject the equation of integrated education with better education. Indeed the separatists treat *Brown* as a paternalistic decision, or less politely, as a racist decision, denigrating blacks in its assumption that all black education means an inferior education. To the separatists a community-directed education, accompanied by real power and adequate resources, seems preferable to compelled integregation—at least for the short run.

A second group, which once might have been classified as liberals, have come to oppose expansion of the concept of discrimination. They are concerned with the apparently broader meaning of *de jure* segregation that the Court has applied; with the breadth of remedial decrees that have been ordered; and—until the Detroit decision—with the possibility that desegregation would become a regional, not district-wide obligation. One needs only to peruse the Congressional debates for the past several years to gain some sense of this shift of political mood; positions once advanced only by southern conservatives have become more widely expressed, 'and more politically acceptable. [The *Bradley* decision, announced several months after the conference, may well diminish the force of these concerns.]

Third, the emerging transformation of discrimination from a concept of color blindness to one of color consciousness, the insistence that color be taken into account affirmatively in order to remedy past discrimination or to secure racial parity in education and employment, have deeply divided old allies, pitting labor against labor, Jewish groups against each other, sparking disputes within the university. Which point of view on any of these issues will prevail—what racial discrimination and the obligation to correct it will come to mean—is impossible to predict.

The other notable development of the decade has been the emergence of non-racial equal educational opportunity issues, premised not on black/white discrimination, but urged by quite different groups, who also claim—with substantial justification—to have been badly treated by the educational system. For the handicapped and retarded youngsters who historically have been denied a public education, equal educational opportunity is viewed as requiring the provision of an education that is, as the opinions in *Mills* and *PARC* suggest, "appropriate" or "suitable" to their needs. If that standard is applied to the severely handicapped, it would necessitate enormous expansion of the government's responsibility to educate and an understanding of education as encompassing not just the three "R's" but also a host of activities designed to take the child from a state of relative dependence to a state of relative independence. For the mildly handicapped, equal educational opportunity is viewed as meaning an end to the consignment to dead-end, inefficacious, stigmatizing special education programs that provide only labels, and indiscernible educational benefits, and substituting serious efforts to offer these children an experience not very different from what "normal" youngsters receive.

For children living in property-poor districts, equal educational opportunity has been defined in terms of the equitable allocation of resources. The claim that such equity—or, as the lawyers put it, "fiscal neutrality"—is constitutionally required was rejected by the Supreme Court in *Rodriguez,* a decision that clearly marks the end of rapid judicial expansion of equal opportunity. But interestingly enough, since *Rodriguez,* the pace of school finance reform has, if anything, increased. In a number of states, including California and New Jersey, courts have struck down school finance systems on state constitutional grounds, insisting on some measure of fairness in the distribution of school dollars. More importantly, legislatures in Kansas, Florida, and Michigan and other states have begun revamping school finance systems in order to accomplish the same end.

And finally, women students in primary and secondary schools are beginning to describe themselves as discriminated against by the schools. Because women in fact do better, in traditional academic terms, than men in primary and secondary school programs, there is a certain irony to that claim. But women can point to policies which exclude them from school programs—athletics, for example; to instances of separate and assertedly unequal treatment; and, most broadly, to school socialization practices that, by assertion, stereotype women, forcing upon them outmoded roles. Some of these arguments—especially those addressed to competitive sports—have prevailed in courts. The greatest push for change is likely to result from Title IX of the 1972 Education Amendments, and the soon-to-be published HEW implementing regulations. Already it is clear that the women's movement has presented—in a very short period of time—a range of issues that, in the racial context, have developed over two decades.

The consequences of this on-going redefinition of equal educational opportunity are hard to estimate precisely. Certain things do seem clear. None of the non-racial equal opportunity issues (treatment of the handicapped, finance reform, treatment of women) seem as emotionally charged, as politically explosive, as does the race question. That is not to say that change is going to be easy, but only to say that I find it hard to imagine politicians standing in school house doors to keep the retarded out of school, or women off the tennis team.

This set of demands—viewed as a whole—is designed to prod the courts into reviewing a host of practices which have historically been viewed as the exclusive domain of educators. The legal agenda for equal educational opportunity, as I have described it, is also in large part the agenda for educational reform of the 1970's. And the hope, at least as expressed by some, is that lawyers and courts can bring about a kind of revolution in education. For several reasons, that hope seems unlikely to come to pass. For one thing, *Rodriguez* is a strong signal that courts are unlikely to be willing participants in bringing about the revolution. They don't want to be super schoolmasters in the name of equal educational opportunity. For another, courts simply cannot raise the money needed to reform schools or oversee the day-to-day activities of schooling that so profoundly and directly affect the lives of children.

One important lesson should be learned from the post-*Brown* experiences with implementing equality of opportunity: a court decision, by itself, cannot secure change; ongoing, sustained political pressure, interest and involvement are needed. Historically, courts have always been a last refuge for groups unable to win battles in the political and legislative arena. That is the strength, the virtue of courts from the point of view of those disadvantaged groups; it also signals the inherent incapacity of courts to produce change on their own.

Equal educational opportunity is, and may always be, an unreachable goal: there is no end to the sentence that begins: "Equal educational opportunity is . . ." It is a concept in flux, and as we come to what may be the end of rapid judicial expansion of the concept, it becomes increasingly important for the reform communities to establish for themselves priorities with respect to these diverse goals. School cannot be non-racist, non-sexist, liberating, open places, providing an equal and appropriate education to an increasingly diverse clientele—at least, it cannot be all of those things at once. Indeed, such goals may be inconsistent with each other in important ways.

Equal educational opportunity is not just a constitutional concept, but a political one as well. Bettering the quality of children's lives in school—the ultimate end of each of these reforms—is not just, or even primarily, a matter of big symbolic court decisions. It also requires slow, tedious political work that must involve not only the courts but also every school district, even every classroom. These patient efforts will get fewer headlines perhaps; they are likely to produce more enduring results. Developing a political strategy that takes these factors into account, that tries to understand what the choices must be to make specific the new equal educational opportunity should be the first item on the political agenda of reform-minded educators and lawyers in the 1970s.

Outlook for the Future

Brian K. Landsberg

The Supreme Court's decision in *Brown v. Board of Education* has two separate but closely related thrusts:
(a) Emphasis on equal educational opportunities;
(b) The requirement that state-imposed racial segregation be eliminated.

The emphasis of most school litigation since *Brown* has, until recently, been on the elimination of state-imposed segregation. I believe this was the correct allocation of legal resources, for at least three reasons. First, the state segregation laws were the clearest violations of *Brown.* Second, while the elimination of state-imposed segregation has not automatically insured equal educational opportunities, the Supreme Court had found it to be a prerequisite to attaining equal educational opportunities. Third, the federal executive focused its efforts on desegregation because that was the focus of Title IV of the Civil Rights Act of 1964.

Brown—A New Phase

Now efforts under *Brown* are entering a new phase. In the states which had laws permitting or requiring segregation, school desegregation is largely an accomplished fact, especially in the rural areas and small cities. There is no longer a focal point for efforts under *Brown;* instead, civil rights lawyers have diffused their litigation into four distinct (though related) areas:
(a) Consolidation of the gains made in the south and repair of the damage which accompanied desegregation.
(b) Expansion of the attack on segregation, both geographically (to

the north) and in terms of the scope of the attack (*e.g.,* relief across district lines or relief covering housing as well as schools).

(c) The beginnings of litigation relating to other aspects of equal educational opportunities, such as fair employment suits against suburban school systems; suits to enforce the rights of non-English speaking children and handicapped children and females to equal access to educational opportunity; suits to ensure that school systems properly implement federal financial assistance programs, such as Title I and the Johnson-O'Malley Act.

(d) A new round of enforcement activity relating to higher education—although the early higher education cases were the foundation upon which *Brown* was built, there has been almost no attempt until recently to develop the law relating to *remedies* for state systems of segregated higher education.

Each of these areas raises difficult issues which were only dimly perceived when *Brown* was decided. In the remainder of my remarks I would like to highlight some of these issues.

Second-Generation Problems

As the South desegregated, black children and educators were confronted by the so-called second-generation problems, such as school closings, classroom segregation, a rise in expulsions and suspensions of students, and a drop in the number of black teachers and principals. Such problems have led civil rights lawyers to seek to draw the courts ever more intimately into the details of the administration of school systems. Where it is possible to fashion fair and uniform rules that do not require the court to substitute its educational or administrative judgment for the judgment of the school authorities, the courts have been responsive—at least when convinced there was a real problem. Examples are the provisions of the *Singleton* case and other cases protecting teachers and administrators in desegregating systems. Most recently, the Department of Justice has obtained appellate court decisions invalidating racially discriminatory uses of the National Teachers Examination in Virginia and South Carolina, and we are now litigating over its use in North Carolina. But in other areas—such as suspensions and expulsions—the courts have so far been less receptive. The civil rights bar must come to grips with this problem: we must search for uniform, fair and workable rules to deal with the second-generation problems, and we must choose strong cases to convince the courts of the need for such rules.

Consolidating the gains—attacking the last bulwarks of segregation in the South—has recently led to a new problem: court battles over who should represent the black community in desegregation litigation. Perhaps this is inevitable in any social movement which has finally achieved a degree of success. So far, however, it is questionable whether black children have benefitted from the split in litigation strategies. The civil rights bar should seek methods of presenting a united front in court.

Brown I had noted that "segregation has long been a nationwide problem, not merely one of sectional concern." Yet the first northern desegregation decision was the *Keyes* case, in 1973. It is clear from the Supreme Court's decision in the *Keyes* case and its indecision in the *Richmond* case that the expansion of the attack on segregation will proceed with deliberate speed—there will be no overnight changes in patterns of urban school segregation, but changes will occur on a case-by-case basis. They are already occurring, in Denver, Pasadena, Pontiac, Indianapolis, Las Vegas, and so on. The Court requires the plaintiffs to make a showing of *de jure* segregation in these cases. One may sympathize with Mr. Justice Powell's question as to whether a child suffers less injury in a *de facto* segregated school than a *de jure* segregated school, but the Court has ruled, and I think our course must be to investigate and litigate each case thoroughly, rather than to rely on the broadbrush approach which was used to establish violations in Southern cases. And, civil rights attorneys must learn to draw fine distinctions—what is the right remedy for one system may not be right for another.

Rodriguez and *Lau*

The first Supreme Court decisions directly relating to aspects of equal educational opportunities other than desegregation were the *Rodriguez* decision last year and the *Lau* decision this year. Both decisions reflect a cautious approach, but in at least the *Lau* decision the approach is forward-looking. The principle established by *Lau,* under Title VI of the Civil Rights Act of 1964, is that school systems enrolling more than a *de minimis* number of non-English speaking children must take steps to assure them equal access to the educational program. *Lau* leaves unanswered a number of questions:

What degree of language disability triggers the obligation?

Does the obligation arise where there is no language disability but where cultural differences tend to exclude minority students?

Is total exclusion the standard?

What remedies are acceptable?

Will the obligation under Title VI be translated into a Fourteenth Amendment obligation?

What are the implications of *Lau* for mentally retarded children?

Finally, private plaintiffs and the federal government have turned their attention back to higher education. The principle of open admissions in public higher education was established in the 1950s and became a reality in the 1960s. The question is whether other vestiges of state-imposed dualism in higher education must be removed—segregated faculties, dual and overlapping curricula, white and black athletic leagues, the proportionately lower enrollment rate of blacks in higher education, and other factors which insure that students choose colleges on a racial basis. The Justice Department, as an intervenor in the Tennessee statewide case and now as plaintiff in the Louisiana statewide higher education case, believes that the law requires that these vestiges be erased. But the question of how to erase them has puzzled the parties and the court in the Tennessee case for several years. It will take all the wisdom that educators and lawyers can muster to work out remedies that are both effective and fair. We must insure that the structure which results from the dismantling of racial dualism provides equally for the needs of the black and white students, teachers, administrators, and communities.

We should not allow the complexity and challenge of these issues to divert us from our efforts to fulfill the promise of *Brown.* But resolution of the issues will require hard thinking and careful fact-gathering on our part. And as the issues mushroom, we will have hard choices to make as to priorities. I think one focus of the discussion which is to follow these presentations this morning should be on what relative priority the various issues mentioned above should be given in allocating the limited resources of the civil rights bar.

A New Look at *Brown*

Ruby G. Martin

I am delighted to be with you this morning, although I must admit that being on the panel with such an array of distinguished, powerful and scholarly gentlemen makes me feel a little like the nervous, newly-appointed woman Assistant Secretary of State, who, at her first press conference when asked what she thought of Red China responded that it's delightful on a beige tablecloth.

A couple of years ago a cartoon appeared in the *New Yorker* Magazine depicting an American Indian father sitting in a teepee reading a bedtime story to his young son. The caption under the cartoon was:

And just then when the battle seemed lost, from beyond the
hills came the welcome sounds of war whoops.

To me, the cartoon said that whether you view salvation as drums, guns and the cavalry blue or war paint, arrows and loin cloth, very much depends upon your ethnic, cultural and social background—where you are coming from. As a prelude to my brief remarks today, I feel it important to take a couple of minutes to explain where I am coming from, lest what I say be misunderstood, misinterpreted, and as has happened, misquoted.

While I have spent most of my adult life as an active proponent of school desegregation (or integration, whatever you prefer), I have, for the last year and a half, stepped away from that particular involvement and have focused my attention, time and energy on the elements and factors that work for or against providing quality education for youngsters in large city school systems, most of which are now overwhelmingly black or brown and poor in terms of their enrollments.

While it is much too early for me to stand up here and talk about "my findings" on these issues because my new experience has been too limited, I am prepared to say that I have concluded that those of us who are genuinely concerned about quality education for minority youngsters not only are guilty of having committed some serious blunders in our legal pursuit of school desegregation during the past twenty years, but are also guilty of grossly misallocating our resources—resources of brains, talent and time over the last ten years. It is this misallocation of resources that concerns me the most.

Most black people under twenty-five years of age have no historical background, appreciation or understanding of *Brown v. Board of Education*. Many believe that the *Brown* case was not initiated by blacks but, rather, that the legal theories and the immediate and long-range goals were developed by whites as the first step in a giant, continuing, well thought out and designed white conspiracy to maintain the status of black people as second-class citizens of this country. If it is difficult for you to comprehend their conspiracy theory, just think, black children born on the day that *Brown* was decided, today are two years out of high school or in their sophomore year in college. And, if they were born in and attended schools in a northern urban area, they probably never attended a school that had any or certainly no more than a handful of white children. These youngsters say to me, "Mrs. Martin, what is all the talk about racial integration, what's so important about that?" In effect, what they say to me is that while you were spending your time and energies trying to desegregate a little school system in Georgia, the school systems of New York City, Chicago, Detroit, Cleveland, Washington, D.C., and every other major city in the nation, were getting blacker and blacker, and the quality of education was getting poorer and poorer. And nobody was doing anything about it. What they say to me, in effect, is that all of you so-called "do gooders" spent one hundred percent of your time trying to desegregate schools, and none of you manifested any concern about us where we are—locked into schools and school systems that were deteriorating physically and educationally at an alarming rate.

Believe me, conversations with these young people have left me shaken and outraged, but somehow hopefully still in control of my faculties.

While I am not yet ready to accept their conspiracy theory, I am prepared to accept the fact that America is not the melting pot we once claimed it to be; ours is a pluralistic society, is likely to remain so, and some of us have an obligation to try to make things better for people where they presently are, and are likely to remain.

I will be frank to admit that accepting the fact that ours is a pluralistic society is going to pose some serious problems. The potential for conflict between the traditional civil rights forces on the one hand and those of us who accept the concept of pluralism is great—and not just philosophically. The potential for conflicts is real because conceptually, the civil rights posture is to view school boards and school administrations as "the enemy" or the other side, if you will, which they certainly were (and still are in some cases). But in 1974, with more and more bankrupt and disintegrating school systems coming under the control of black school boards and black school administrations, I believe we have an obligation to re-think that posture and devise strategies and programs that try to deal with school boards and school administrations as friends as well as enemies. I believe that the conflicts will be lessened if we are honest and communicate. I stress the importance of communication and understanding and honesty because it is important that conflict be avoided.

For example, if the new Elementary and Secondary Education Act, which is being debated in the House is passed in any form, an open conflict is likely to occur. It is likely to occur because some of us who campaigned for tight and rigid guidelines under the old Act to protect poor youngsters from so-called "bad" or unsympathetic superintendents and school boards this time will be campaigning for guidelines to give "good" or sympathetic superintendents and boards what they say they need—more flexibility in the use of Title I funds in trying to provide quality education for urban youngsters. The potential conflict will be lessened if we can agree on some basic facts, perhaps the most important of which is who are our clients, where are they located, and what relief is likely to have the greatest affirmative impact on their individual lives.

According to the most recent statistics, there are now more black school children in urban school systems than in rural ones and these school systems are being administered more and more by people of good will. Those of us who seek to provide quality education for black youngsters through the courts must seek the advice and counsel of school officials and administrators of good will who have the same goals.

Perhaps most important, from my point of view, is the need for more of us to get involved in the nuts and bolts of dealing with the here and now factors that mitigate against urban youngsters being afforded an equal educational opportunity—the growing strength of teachers' unions, the governing structure of school systems, the financing of school systems, developing measures of accountability, and the like.

I wish to stress that I am not advocating separatism or urging an abandonment of school desegregation litigation or federal administration enforcement of Title VI (if Title VI has not already been administratively repealed). What I am saying is that there is a need for more of us to turn our attention to trying to provide equal educational opportunities for black youngsters where they are and are likely to remain for their entire school careers.

A couple of weeks ago, I was at an elementary school in Washington and a fifth grader came up to me and said, "Mrs. Martin, do you know what will happen to you if you don't pay your exorcist bill?" She said, "You get repossessed." Maybe what has happened to me during the last year and a half is that I have been repossessed. Whatever has happened, I know that if I could undo some of the things that I did as the Director of HEW's Office for Civil Rights, I would. I believe now that no school district should ever be desegregated without the people who will be directly affected by the process having a voice in determining how that process should proceed. No black school should ever be closed in the name of desegregation without a thorough analysis of the impact of the closing on the total life of the black community surrounding it. (Look at what is happening to the availability of higher education for blacks in the south under the guise of desegregation.) No school desegregation case should ever be filed unless the relief sought has been thought out and analyzed in the most minute detail and the plaintiffs agree that the relief is in their best interest.

While I hope that I have not been either possessed in the first instance or repossessed for non-payment, I do feel stronger than ever that unless some of us turn our talents toward dealing with the here and now and accept the pluralism that is a fact of life in America, the next twenty years will see the total destruction of public education in this country. My young friends with the conspiracy theory would say that my predictions will come to pass because they are simply part of that giant conspiracy. I hope they are wrong.

Chicanos and Equal Educational Opportunity

Vilma S. Martinez

In 1944, in Hudsbeth County, Texas, a nineteen-year old Chicano was convicted of murder and sentenced to death.[1] This was not unusual except for the fact that the boy was blind, was mentally retarded, was retaliating for an attack on his father, and was physically unable—under the applicable criminal statute—to have the necessary intent to justify a finding of first degree murder. In spite of the fact that more than fifty percent of the county's population was Chicano, no Chicano had ever served on a jury. On appeal, attorneys for the boy cited a 1900 case, *Carter v. Texas*[2] in which the Texas Supreme Court had held that blacks could not be excluded from juries.[3] In this case, however, the court distinguished *Carter,* holding that the Fourteenth Amendment did not extend to Chicanos. Due to a lack of funds, no appeal was made to the United States Supreme Court, and the boy was executed later that year.

The anomalous position of the Chicano—not white, yet not, in old-style parlance, "colored"—has been one of the roots of the Chicano tragedy in this country. It has produced a history of legal struggle for equal educational opportunity that has been as difficult as, but at the same time significantly different from, that waged by black Americans.

In 1930, Chicanos argued *Salvatierra v. Independent School District,*[4] a case in which the Supreme Court ultimately denied a writ of certiorari.[5] Attorneys for the Chicano community contended that separate schools for Chicanos existed without authority since Chicanos were "other whites." The trial court issued an injunction forbidding segregation of Chicanos, but the Texas Court of Civil Appeals dissolved the injunction because Mexican-race students had language difficulties which could best be solved in separate schools. That Chicanos argued that they were "other white" is not surprising in light of the fact that other minority groups in the United States had made similar arguments, and in fact were probably motivated by a Supreme Court decision three years prior to *Salvatierra–Gong Lum v. Rice,*[6] a case concerning a Chinese. There the United States Supreme Court upheld the Mississippi Supreme Court interpretation of the distinction between "white" and "colored" as dividing "the educable children into those of the pure white or Caucasian race, on the one hand, and the brown, yellow, and black races on the other hand . . ."[7] For a similar black strategy one should read C. Vose, *Caucasians Only,*[8] a documentation of Thurgood Marshall's arguments in *Shelley v. Kraemer,*[9] the restrictive covenants case.

A Historical Perspective of the Evolution of Chicano Education

To clearly understand our place in time, we need a historical perspective of the evolution of Chicano education. Initially, school districts were directed by the mandates of the 1876 Texas Constitution[10] which provided that: "Separate schools shall be provided for the white and colored children and impartial provision shall be made for both." Left to their own interpretations, school board officials applied a righteous strict constructionalism: any fool knew what "colored" and "white" meant—Mexicans, of course, were neither. Thus school districts such as El Paso and Nueces Counties, which were among those with the highest concentrations of Chicanos in the nation, did not provide any schooling at all for Chicanos.

At the turn of the century, school district policies lacked consistency because all followed the theory that elected bodies could be final arbiters of constitutional requirements. But they were faced with a dilemma—some semblance of education had to be provided, but where—the black or the white schools? Thus, Chicanos were forced into a limbo of separate schools without the sanction of state statute, but under the aegis of state law. Chicano segregation, a peculiar institution rooted in local government law, was a hybrid school segregation that existed as long as Southern black segregation. Thus, for example, the Seguin school board established separate Mexican schools in the summer of 1902. Other districts like Kingsville reaffirmed and formalized the inviolable policy in a school board meeting in 1929: "not to allow any Mexican to attend Flato school, but to attend Stephen F. Austin school, where 'special arrangements' were made for teaching."[11]

The separate system in the early twentieth century was inferior not only in a psychological sense but in a very physical sense as well. In 1927 in San Juan, Texas, the San Juan grammar school teachers were allocated triple the wages of San Juan Mexican school teachers, even though they taught comparable grades and the Mexican school was double the size of the Anglo school. Even the provision of noninstructional needs was a disgrace. For example, in the Pharr-San Juan-Alamo, Texas District of 1928, the Mexican classrooms were grossly overcrowded; yet in that year the school board minutes reflect that "upon motion made, seconded, and adopted there was voted an amount equal to twenty dollars per room for Mexican schools and thirty dollars for American schools per room, for playground equipment."[12] Even toys for children were allocated by deliberate school board policy on the basis of race.

But the most grotesque features of the separate Mexican school system remain virtually unknown. An HEW on-site review of Pecos, Texas in 1969 documented what our parents have always known: "Prior to 1938, no Mexican-American had attended junior or senior high school . . . According to reliable community contacts, before this time there was a policy of not permitting Mexican-Americans to go beyond the sixth grade." Indeed the historical exclusion of Chicanos from public education beyond the elementary grades until 1948 was a finding of fact in *Perez v. Sonora Independent School District.*[13] In 1942-43, Wilson Little, an educator commissioned by the Texas Department of Education, found that between ninety and one hundred percent of all Mexican children in Texas schools were in the elementary grades.

The trauma of World War II brought demands for change. Out of this holocaust the GI Forum was born, its genesis lying in the death of a Chicano World War II hero—Felix Longoria. When Three Rivers, Texas refused to have this Chicano buried in its whites-only cemetery, Longoria was buried in Arlington Cemetery, and inspired the hopes of millions of Chicanos for a real share of the American dream. Dr. Hector Garcia, whom Father Hesburgh and other members of the commission must remember as an active former member of the U.S. Commission on Civil Rights, founded the GI Forum and began a crusade against discrimination. But the changes still reflected two facts. First, few, if any, in the educational and political power structure understood, or even made attempts to understand, the existence and special role of Chicanos as a distinct ethnic and cultural group; and second, explicit segregation by ethnic group was still the law of the land. The few successes in courts were, therefore, not on grounds of equal protection, but on the basis of denial of due process.

In 1946, a California federal district court in *Westminster v. Mendez*[14] held separate schools for Chicanos violative of due process since they were not provided for by state law—the Ninth Circuit affirmed in 1947. In 1948, in *Delgado,* a Texas federal district court enjoined school districts in four counties as well as the state superintendent from segregating Mexican children—again on due process grounds. *Delgado v. Bastrop Independent School District*[15]; accord, *Gonzales v. Sheely*.[16] Thus, prior to *Brown v. Board of Education,*[17] there had been a series of both federal court and administrative decisions effectively proscribing the segregation of Chicanos.

When *Brown* came down in 1954 it eliminated the need for Chicanos to continue arguing for an end to segregation on due process grounds (which of course had been necessary because *Plessy v. Ferguson*[18] sanctioned explicit segregation). After *Brown* it was clear that all racial groups had to be treated equally, and segregation was inherently unequal. But now school districts willingly relented to the Chicano due process arguments and argued Chicanos had not been covered by state statutes authorizing segregation; thus there was no *de jure* segregation as to Chicanos and *a fortiori* no need for desegregation because of tainted state action.

On the same day that *Brown* was handed down, the Court cleared the way for a Chicano equal protection argument in *Hernandez v. Texas*[19] where the Supreme Court found that Mexican-Americans constituted a separate group for purposes of full protection under the Fourteenth Amendment. Thus, the flurry of executions by all-Anglo juries in Texas stopped, and again in the death of one line of cases there was born a new theory of law. While some Chicano attorneys retained the worn due process argument, the merging of the two theories was most dramatically completed in *Cisneros v. Corpus Christi Ind. School District.*[20] In *Cisneros* the Fifth Circuit held that segregation of Chicanos in Corpus Christi schools was unconstitutional on the basis of *Brown.*

But if *Cisneros* heralded the advent of a new era, it also sounded the first alarm of concomitant problems. In the hiatus between *Delgado* and *Cisneros, Brown* and its progeny had developed a set of rules with a particularly black perspective. The question is now whether rules which are formulated to protect southern blacks are applicable by extension to Chicanos. For example, the *Singleton* ratio *(Singleton v. Jackson Municipal Separate School District)*[21] is a laudable effort to protect black teachers and integrate schools by distributing black teachers in a manner that would leave no racially identifiable schools. In the Singleton case, the court stipulated that the district shall assign principals, teachers, teacher-aides, and other staff who work directly with the children so that the ratio of Negro to white teachers in each school, and the ratio of other staff in each, are substantially the same as each such ratio is to the teachers and other staff, respectively, in the entire school system. But, as the Fifth Circuit recognized in *United States v. Texas*[22] (Austin Independent School District), a Singleton ratio may make sense in the milieu of school districts having large numbers of black teachers, but made absolutely no sense in the southwest context where the proportion of Chicano teachers does not begin to approximate the proportion of Chicano students. Judge Wisdom astutely observed that a *Singleton* ratio preoccupation was a subterfuge for the real problem—hiring. Moreover, the *Singleton* ratio may work at odds with the Chicano need for bilingual education.

Bilingual-bicultural education may itself be at odds with *Brown* and its progeny if the latter are strictly construed. Although it would be a great accomplishment to have integrated bilingual classes, this may not always be possible because there may not be a sufficient number of Anglo parents willing to put their children in bilingual classes. English-as-a-second-language (ESL) classes which work at part time integration, do accomplish that, but have failed educationally. True bilingual-bicultural education classes may at times call for separate classes in substantive subjects though hopefully not on separate campuses. Educational achievement among Chicanos is a testimony to the deplorable means utilized to educate Chicano children today.

In *Lau v. Nichols* the Supreme Court recognized that something needs to be done to remedy the deficiencies of the educational system with regard to Chicanos. But Justice Douglas was obscure as to just what Title VI and that May 25th Memorandum may require.[23] It is our fear that the decision may be taken as a tacit acceptance of ESL classes, which have so far been a dramatic failure. Our position is that ESL classes represent everything that the Court found so abhorrent in *Lau:* an uncomprehending child as a captive audience. Moreover, *Brown* and its progeny taught us that the only acceptable plan is "one that works."[24] Educators should be bound to no lesser standard in providing equal educational opportunity to Chicanos. The *Serna v. Portales* case which I argued before the Tenth Circuit on March 20, 1974 is an expansion of *Lau* in that it substitutes a constitutional mandate for bilingual education for a statutory one.

While our line of cases may have different roots from those brought in the interest of black students, it is evident that our efforts are often inextricably interwoven and that Chicanos and blacks can frequently combine their efforts. Such was the case in *Diana v. Calif. Board of Education,*[25] and *Larry P. v. Riles,*[26] two recent California cases dealing with the Educable Mentally Retarded misclassification. In the first instance the tenor of the prejudice was shown to be linguistic; in the second, racial. It is my sincere hope that this splendid cooperation between our two peoples and between all peoples may continue to the betterment of mankind.

[1] *Sanchez v. State,* 147 Tex. Crim. 436, 181 S.W. 2d 87 (1944).

[2] 177 U.S. 442.

[3] *Sanchez v. State,* 156 Tex. Crim. 468, 243 S.W. 2d 700 (1951).

[4] 33 S.W. 2d 790 (Tex. Civ. App., 4th Dist., 1930).

[5] *Cert. denied,* 284 U.S. 580 (1931).

[6] 275 U.S. 78, 80 (1972).

[7] Mississippi Constitution of 1890, S 207.

[8] University of California Press (1967), pp. 83-84, 129-31.

[9] 334 U.S. 1 (1948).

[10] Article VII, S 7.

[11] U.S. Department of Health, Education, and Welfare, *On-Site Review of Kingsville ISD,* June 23-24, 1971.

[12] Pharr-San Juan-Alamo Board Minutes, Vol. II, p. 117 (March 10, 1928).

[13] Civil No. 6-224 (N.D. Tex., No. 5, 1970).

[14] 161 F. 2d 774 (Ninth Cir., 1947).

[15] Civil No. 388 (W.D. Tex., June 15, 1948).

[16] 96 F. Supp. 1004 (D. Ariz., 1951).

[17] 347 U.S. 483 (1934).

[18] 163 U.S. 537 (1896).

[19] 347 U.S. 475.

[20] 324 F. Supp. 599 (S.D. Tex., 1970), *cert. denied* 413 U.S. 920.

[21] 419 F. 2d 1211, 1217-18 (Fifth Cir., 1970), *cert. denied* 402 U.S. 943 (1971).

[22] Civil No. A-70-CA-80 (W.D. Tex., June 28, 1971).

[23] Editor's note: The author refers here to Title VI of the 1964 Civil Rights Act and to the May 25th, 1970 Memorandum (35 Fed. Reg. 11595) HEW issued on that date. The Memorandum was sent to schools with more than five percent national origin minority children. It was a clarification of the regulations under Title VI concerned with children having language disabilities.

[24] *Kemp v. Beasley,* 389 F. 2d 178 (1968).

[25] CA NOC-70 37 RFP (N.D. Cal Feb.).

[26] 343 F. Supp. 1306 (N.D. Calif., 1972).

Desegregation at Midpoint

Gary Orfield

Americans are impatient for rapid solutions to basic social problems, neat inventive answers that resolve the difficulties without any great turmoil or inconvenience. Priding themselves on their pragmatism, liberals are often prepared to admit that last year's program "failed" and to enthusiastically endorse another simple answer. The school desegregation battle has been taking too long and it has been too much hard work. People tend to forget what it is all about. When they see that all educational problems do not vanish once black and white children sit together, they announce that "integration has failed." Wondering if it is all worthwhile, they look for an easier answer.

I begin with the assumption that the United States Supreme Court was right—that there is no other answer. A caste system of separate schools in a society with pervasive racial inequality does produce inherently unequal schools—not because there is something wrong with black children but because there is a basic defect in the society. Integrated systems create the possibility of real equality.

No change in basic social arrangements comes easily. If we really believe that race is the most fundamental issue in American society and that the public schools are the crucial institution both for transmission of American culture and for mobility in social and economic status, we must expect that a long, intense, and sustained effort will be necessary to change the treatment of the country's minority groups within its most important public institutions.

Although civil rights supporters are much more accustomed to describing continuing problems gravely, it is essential now that we recognize the vast accomplishments of the twenty-year effort in the south and that we admit that we have had workable principles of law for accomplishing any significant northern desegregation only very recently. Much of the discouragement with school integration comes from the constantly recurring assumption that northern segregation has persisted in spite of a long effort to enforce desegregation law there.

The statistics show that, outside the largest cities, we are nearing the end of a remarkable process of reorganizing the basic structure of southern education. Civil rights enforcement has changed at least the external contours of most southern school systems. The battle in hundreds of communities and thousands of schools is now one of adapting the internal operation of individual schools to their changed student bodies, moving from desegregation to integration.

Contrary to announcements about the failure of integration, and in spite of the best efforts of President Nixon and the great executive agencies to impede the process, the proportion of southern blacks attending predominantly white schools has increased from about one percent, when President Kennedy sent his civil rights bill to Congress, to forty-five percent by fall, 1972. While ninety-nine percent of southern blacks attended completely segregated schools in 1963, only seven percent did nine years later.

When you remember that the great majority of southern school systems were totally segregated in 1963, that the strongest court orders of the time were calling only for grade-a-year token integration through freedom of choice, and that the 1964 Civil Rights Act was seriously enforced for only three years before the election of President Nixon, the abolition of dual school systems in much of the south is one of the impressive social accomplishments of American history.

Perhaps the most encouraging thing about desegregation in the south is the fact that it is now widely accepted as a matter of fact. In spite of the bitter busing controversies, each successive study of public opinion in the south shows growing acceptance of desegregation and growing willingness of southern whites to have their children in schools with substantial numbers of black students. In several areas the south has even achieved reasonably stable metropolitan-wide desegregation.

Outside the rural south, segregation of blacks is primarily a problem of urbanized areas. Although it is now two decades since the *Brown* decision, it is only three years since the Supreme Court's first basic treatment of the issue of southern urban segregation in the *Swann* case. It is less than a year since the *Keyes* case brought the first Supreme Court pronouncement on segregation in cities outside of the south with its overt history of official segregation. The fact that a conservative Supreme Court has begun to establish some workable principles of urban desegregation law should be counted as a major achievement.

Of equal importance has been the sudden recognition by the Supreme Court of the legal rights of the nation's second largest minority—children from a Spanish language background. Only last year, the Supreme Court held that Chicanos have a constitutional right to desegregated schools. Just weeks ago, the Supreme Court, in the *Lau* case, sustained HEW's claim that the 1964 Civil Rights Act requires school systems to devise educational plans which meet the critical needs of non-English speaking students who are normally simply ignored by school officials. Although this decision concerned Chinese-American students, its most dramatic effect will be on Mexican Americans and Puerto Ricans.

These very new principles of law have barely begun to make themselves felt. The courts, however, have taken two crucial steps in adapting a body of desegregation law shaped to deal with the simpler social context of the south to the much more complicated ethnic patterns of large northern and western cities.

The Scale of the Problem

When we talk about school desegregation, most of us have some mental image we use to visualize the problem. In the late 50s the image was one of the children in Little Rock going into Central High School surrounded by jeering crowds, and protected by federal troops. Today, when most people think of desegregating northern and western school systems, they tend to visualize the endless expanses of ghetto communities in New York or Chicago and to see the jeering crowds in Canarsie or the burned-out buses in Pontiac. The problem with these images, of course, is that they vastly distort the immensely complex diversity of the country. One result is that people tend to seriously overestimate the scale of the problem of urban desegregation. In fact, a great deal of school desegregation can be accomplished in the north and west without great cost and within the boundaries of established principles of law.

School segregation in the north and west is a far more localized problem than most people realize. Most states outside the south have relatively few minority students and can easily desegregate. In spite of the national frenzy over busing, only six northern states and no western state had as many as a tenth black students in 1970. The vast majority, 94.3 percent, of the country's black pupils are concentrated in twenty-three states and the District of

Columbia. Most of these are southern and border states. In twenty-two of the northern and western states, blacks average only two percent of the total enrollment.

Other groups of minority students are even more localized. The 2.8 million Spanish-surnamed, Asian, and Indian students are concentrated in nine states, with almost seventy percent in just three states—California, Texas, and New York.[1]

Ninety-three percent of blacks and eighty-eight percent of Spanish origin students go to school in one-fourth of the country's school districts. Almost sixty percent of white children, on the other hand, go to school in districts where minority enrollment averages only two percent.

The localization of the problem of segregation creates special problems in areas of extreme minority concentration, but it also has seldom-discussed political consequences. A substantial majority of members of the Senate and the House, for instance, represent constituencies where there is literally almost no one to bus. This fact, and the fact that the desegregation process affects only limited numbers of communities at a time, may greatly diminish the political pressures on the courts, particularly once desegregation is successfully accomplished in a number of northern cities and the passions stirred in the 1972 campaign settle.

Big central city school systems pose the greatest difficulties for desegregation, but many of these systems are neither so vast, nor so segregated, nor so important to minority children as popular stereotypes suggest. The 1970 Census showed only twenty-six communities in the United States with more than 100,000 black residents. The public schools in these communities enrolled 2.4 million black students, about thirty-six percent of the national black enrollment. Slightly more than half these cities had black elementary enrollments over fifty percent, and thus were clearly becoming majority black systems. Only six of these large systems were outside the south. The majority black systems contained slightly more than a fifth of all black students.

Obviously, desegregation poses the greatest problems in these cities. The problem, however, is not on the scale of that in New York City. The New York system is twice as big as the next largest system and about ten times as big as the tenth largest system in the United States.

Substantial numbers of whites remain in most of the predominantly black systems. There is a possibility of devising desegregation plans for elements of school systems even if the courts won't face the metropolitan issue and a city-wide plan isn't feasible. Some systems are organized into constituent units which may provide targets for desegregation actions. The recent successful NAACP litigation against segregation in one of New York City's decentralized districts might establish a precedent for such actions.

Even in the cities with the largest black communities total desegregation is sometimes possible within the central city boundaries. A substantial majority of the hundred largest school districts in the United States have less than forty percent combined black and Spanish-surname enrollment. If the civil rights organizations can find the necessary resources or federal agencies the needed commitment, these systems can be desegregated without any more Supreme Court decisions.

Central city districts as a whole account for a declining fraction of the nation's educational system. In some areas, in fact, their proportion of local black students is already falling. Between 1970 and 1972, for example, the absolute number of black students fell in several city systems, including St. Louis, New Orleans, and Newark. In others, such as Philadelphia and Washington, there was no significant growth in black central city enrollment even though the number of black children in the metropolitan area was rising.

The vast majority of the country's black and Mexican-American students go to school in districts where desegregation in schools with majorities of English-speaking whites is possible. These include a number of metropolitan districts, and suburban systems which are receiving large numbers of minority students.

The widespread stereotype of black cities surrounded by a noose of white suburbs often obscures the growing potential for suburban desegregation. Few realize, for example, that the largest school system in the United States is the Washington suburban district of Prince George's County [Maryland], a system containing more black children than Pittsburgh, Boston, or Richmond. It was desegregated by a court order in early 1973. Ft. Lauderdale, Florida, is much more widely known for its pleasant beach than for its role as the center of a metropolitan school district which also serves more black children than any of these three major cities. Court orders brought eighty percent of these students into predominantly white schools in 1971.

The school systems of inner suburbs will surely be a crucial focus for the desegregation struggle in the next few years. In some metropolitan areas, the movement of black population out across the city line has already assumed large proportions. Statistics in a number of regions show surprising numbers of black students already in suburban systems.

While Chicago, for example, contains the nation's largest continuous ghetto, its metropolitan area also has more black children in suburban classrooms than the entire black enrollment in Gary, Indiana. The Los Angeles suburbs contain more black students than the Newark schools. San Francisco Bay Area suburban systems enroll more black children than the city of San

Francisco, and almost as many as Oakland. Although Washington, D.C. is often cited as the case proving the utter futility of desegregation efforts, more than a third of the black children in the metropolitan area were in suburban systems by 1972, and their numbers were rising rapidly. The Washington suburbs had almost as many black pupils as Atlanta, the nation's second largest predominantly black city. The suburbs will certainly be increasingly important to black students in the future.

Suburban systems are already even more important for other minority groups. In more than a third of the metropolitan areas with substantial numbers of minority students, Spanish-surnamed pupils are either equally distributed between city and suburbs or actually more likely to be in the suburbs. Even in some of the communities with the largest Chicano settlements, there is relatively little concentration in the central city. In Los Angeles there are almost as many students in the suburbs; in San Diego there are more. The figures are about equal in El Paso and Albuquerque.

As population movements continue, the problem of suburban desegregation will be an increasingly serious one both for minority families searching for a first step out of the ghetto or barrio and for whites wondering how far to run. In a sense, the problem may become even more urgent for inner suburbs than for central cities. Unlike city residents, residents of older suburbs are seldom held by proximity to work, old tight-knit neighborhood ties, or cultural institutions. They have the financial resources to move more readily than inner city whites. Most suburbs are so small that there is nowhere to flee to within the jurisdiction.

Realtors often exacerbate the suburban problem by targeting integrated communities for sales to minority buyers only. This creates a self-fulfilling prophecy of ghettoization. While busing opponents often say they would prefer to solve the whole problem through housing integration, the fact is that suburban housing integration is probably almost impossible to maintain without some convincing guarantee that schools will remain integrated. Similarly, action on the school issue must be accompanied by group action against housing discrimination. Neither school nor housing desegregation may be achieved in isolation.

Unless we act, we face not only the prospect of decaying central cities, occupied largely by minority groups and elderly whites, but also a new ring of decaying transitional suburbs, which will mock the dreams of the rising black middle class. This is already happening outside Newark, where the metropolitan area now contains four smaller school systems dominated by minority students, and some blacks are leaving for a second set of suburbs. This underlines a seldom discussed fact, the black middle class searching for middle-class schools are principal victims of urban segregation. Unfortunately, effective suburban desegregation will often raise issues about school district boundary lines in the suburbs similar to the questions already raised about the legitimacy of the boundaries between the cities and the suburbs. (Even if the Supreme Court turns back the Detroit issue it will recur in another form.)

Even if the current Supreme Court denies metropolitan-wide desegregation efforts, there must be a continuing drive to win some sort of enforcement procedure permitting crossing of school district lines. The inescapable fact is that all central city and segregated suburban systems are in metropolitan areas with large majorities of English-speaking whites. In some of these areas, metropolitan desegregation could be accomplished at a low cost and without much inconvenience. This was the case in Richmond, Virginia, for example, where an evenly divided Supreme Court stalemated on a case which would have consolidated the three school districts in a relatively compact metropolitan area. Even if the courts did not consolidate districts or insist on perfect racial and ethnic balance in every school, the maintenance of desegregated educational systems could be greatly enhanced by the development of some mechanism to exchange substantial numbers of students across district lines, thus providing some assurance of stable integration.

The feasibility of a metropolitan approach to desegregation is already being tested in several areas where country-wide school systems exist. Eighteen of the hundred largest districts in the country already contain both a city and the surrounding urban county. The existence of such districts has made possible metropolitan-wide desegregation plans in such scattered locations as Las Vegas, Nevada; Nashville, Tennessee; Greenville, South Carolina; Charlotte-Mecklenburg, North Carolina; and most Florida cities. Early experience shows that metropolitan plans can frequently be carried out, even in extremely difficult political circumstances, without massive white flight.

The first significant study of these districts is underway in Florida, where researchers have followed the attitudes of 6000 parents in eight desegregated county systems. The scholars at Florida Atlantic University report that most were willing to accept integration, except where newly bused children were sent more than ten miles to predominantly black schools. Five of the eight districts actually gained white enrollment in fall 1972, at the height of a year of bitter state and national political controversy over busing. Significant losses of white students were limited to counties where the metropolitan area actually sprawled out across county lines.

The Florida study showed that the real problem was not busing. More than forty percent of students leaving for private schools were not scheduled to be bused to public schools. While a fourth of them would have walked to their desegregated public school, ninety percent of them had to ride in a bus or car to their new private school, which was much more likely to be over ten miles from their home. Yet about a third of the parents of transferring children said they were worried about their child's safety in the new school, and forty-one percent expressed worries about the buses, even though they now became much more reliant on vastly more dangerous private automobile transportation. An overwhelming majority were unimpressed by the school's academic program.

Contrary to their expectations, the researchers found no "tipping point" even in a predominantly black county system. They found, in fact, that most parents were willing to send their children to predominantly black schools so long as they were not subjected at the same time to a new lengthy bus ride.

It is vitally important to remember, in examining statistics about white flight, that a decline in white enrollment in central cities and even in many suburbs is now the natural result of the age structure, distribution, and family plans of white families in metropolitan areas. Central city school systems are losing white students at appreciable rates even when there are virtually no minority students or no desegregation plan in operation. If one compares the experience of desegregated cities with similar segregated or overwhelmingly white cities, one finds that much of what local educators and politicians describe as white flight is simply a totally predictable decline in enrollment, quite unrelated to desegregation.

Even though there may be no specific tipping point, the high level of stable integration observed in a number of the metropolitan plans, contrasted to the rapid desegregation in some of the less successful central city plans, such as those in Richmond and Norfolk, strongly underlines the urgency of a continued search for means of enforcing metropolitan remedies.

The Demands of Complexity

Even a brief discussion of the diversity and complexity of urban desegregation suggests the staggering growth in the difficulty of achieving successful judicial enforcement in moving from the rural south to the urban north. There is need for expert consideration of issues of demography, governmental structure, housing patterns, bilingualism, transportation, and educational administration. The proof of official responsibility for segregation is many times more difficult than in the south and the problem of shaping an adequate remedy is of a wholly new order of magnitude. These demands have swamped the capacities of private civil rights organizations. The result is that relatively few cases are energetically pursued and the judges often must make decisions based on inadequate data in the cases that are decided.

Real movement on the issues in the north and west probably requires commitment of some of the enforcement resources of the federal government. With funds and manpower to do the necessary investigations and to help school systems shape remedies reasonably likely to work, and with the powerful sanction of federal fund cutoff reinforcing the threat of litigation, the balance might begin to shift in favor of substantial desegregation in the north. If this effort were reinforced by a substantial expansion of the Emergency School Assistance program to permit a visible upgrading of school systems when they desegregate and federal assumption of the controversial costs of busing, the transition could be greatly eased.

In an extraordinary decision, *Adams v. Richardson,* a unanimous Court of Appeals, sitting en banc, found HEW guilty of intentionally subverting the 1964 Civil Rights Act as it affected southern school systems and state systems of higher education. The courts denied all the normal and legitimate defenses of necessary administrative discretion because the record was so unambiguous. The record of HEW in the north is even worse, with the sum total of only one fund cutoff—to the tiny suburb of Ferndale, Michigan—in nine years of enforcement. Title VI clearly requires HEW either to cut off federal funds or to employ some other effective method of ending unconstitutional segregation in school systems receiving federal aid. This law is being violated on a monumental scale—a Watergate-era scale.

In the meantime, HEW is employing its steadily growing enforcement staff on a wide diversity of secondary issues. There are extensive investigations of the issue of unequal educational programs, particularly for Spanish-speaking children, investigations and negotiations which are normally based on a separate but equal conception, not a theory of integrated, bilingual, bicultural education. In fact some of the "comprehensive educational plans" that HEW has been accepting rest on the improbable assumption that you can provide equal bilingual instruction in segregated monolingual schools.

Twenty years after *Brown* the south has profoundly changed. The fashionable thing today is to ignore the impact of school desegregation and attribute the change to the Voting Rights Act and the rise of black electoral power. To some degree this explanation is surely true, but we can't forget that the law covered only six states and had no impact at all on some of the states where change has been most dramatic. In fact, the rise in black voting strength has been more than matched in the south by an increase in white registrations, and the black turnout rate is low. Even more important is the fact that the vote would make relatively little difference as long as the public was prepared to respond to the classic tradition of southern politics—racial polarization.

This tactic has been defeated in a number of states, I am convinced, only because segregation has been defeated, and people have discovered that their fears and stereotypes were wrong. The realization that school desegregation was inevitable and the discovery that nothing horrible happened were of elemental social and political importance. Polarization was always most extreme when change threatened but leaders could still claim it could be stopped and was illegitimate.

The pioneers of the school desegregation movement took on a seemingly impossible and endless struggle because they realized its fundamental social importance. If we are to avoid a staggering level of racial separation in the metropolitan complexes which now dominate American life, there is no choice but to pursue a similarly difficult struggle.

An Appeal for Unity

Arthur J. Goldberg

We meet at a time of profound cynicism and disillusionment about our government, its leaders and the political process. This cynicism is understandable. Watergate has shocked this nation and rightly so. Watergate involves allegations and evidence before Congressional committees and before courts that high officials of our government authorized and participated in illegal bugging, illegal disruption of the political process, perjury, political favoritism influencing governmental decision-making, violation of the election laws, cover-up and obstruction of justice and misprision of felony.

Two former cabinet officers are now standing trial for certain of these offenses. Several former White House officials have already pleaded guilty to various Watergate crimes. Other former high-ranking government officials are under indictment.

Those charged, but not convicted, are entitled to the presumption of innocence, but it cannot be gainsaid that the ever-mounting disclosures have eroded public confidence in the leadership of our country.

Cynicism and discouragement likewise permeate the civil rights movement. It is only honest to admit this.

There are adherents of civil rights who say that the great promise of *Brown*[1] has not been fully realized. In this, they are right; but they are not right in "copping out"; the struggle to overcome centuries of racial discrimination in so many aspects of American life is bound to be arduous and frustrating. Thomas Paine aptly warned that: "Those who expect to reap the blessings of freedom must ... undergo the fatigue of supporting it." There are civil rights adherents who say that in *Brown* the Court was initially right in holding that separate can never be equal but that since equality is still denied, let us return to separatism, for at least by so doing we can preserve our pride and safeguard our identity. I understand this reaction and am a firm believer in a pluralistic society rather than a homogenized one. But the goal of an integrated and desegregated public education decreed by *Brown,* is worthy of our continuing efforts and must not be abandoned because of fatigue and discouragement.

There are those who despair that the struggle for human rights seems to be ever enduring and never ending; that it is too much to expect continuing pursuit of Martin Luther King's dream when the dream appears to be far from reality. To these, I would say, to paraphrase Tennyson, more things are wrought by dreams than this world conceives of.

There are those, formerly part of the great coalition that forged *Brown* [2] who now fear that *Brown,* carried to its logical conclusion, in seeking to eliminate racial discrimination against blacks in education, will do so at the expense of other racial and ethnic minorities who, too, have suffered grievous discrimination. To these adherents of civil rights who have expressed these fears and concerns, most recently in briefs filed in the *DeFunis*[3] case, I would say, you are misguided in your fears and are wrong, simply wrong. To eliminate the vestiges of slavery, as promised by the Thirteenth Amendment—to seek to correct an injustice existing since the very foundation of this country—is a moral and constitutional obligation of transcendent importance.

It is understandable that victims of past discrimination in educational opportunity react against the specter of the imposition of quotas. The fact is, however, that no responsible adherent of civil rights is proposing the restoration of a quota system—the infamous numerus clausus.[4] The affirmative action program of seeking to admit a moderate—indeed, a modest—number of black students to law schools and other institutions of higher learning is an essential element in a program to correct an historic inequity; it is not a program to establish a quota system for admission of students to institutions of higher education.

All agree that some form of affirmative action is required, but some overlook the teaching of *Brown* that the most effective type of affirmative action program to overcome past injustices is for black students to share an educational experience with other students by admission to their ranks.[5] Preparatory courses are useful but actual admission to an integrated classroom provides real educational benefits to white and black students alike.

There is a clear and present danger that the fissure in the civil rights coalition evident in the *DeFunis* case will widen and extend to the busing and other difficult cases which are coming to the courts for adjudication.[6] This would be a matter of very great regret.

There is perhaps an even greater danger, division in the great coalition in the Supreme Court of the United States established in *Brown* and persisting in *Brown's* progeny. *Brown* itself was a unanimous decision[7] and, during the Warren era[8] all school desegregation cases were also unanimous.[9]

But the Court, as presently constituted, for the first time since *Brown,* has begun to divide on certain issues involving desegregation of public education.[10]

If this greatest of coalitions disintegrates, this would be most tragic. A civil rights coalition may urge; the Supreme Court decides. And, equally important, the Supreme Court is often the moral conscience of the nation. It was in *Brown*; it should remain so with the authority which unanimity provides.

Brown, as all historians of the Supreme Court agree, is one of its most significant decisions. One of the reasons is that *Brown* transcended the momentous issue of integrating public education. *Brown* had a profound impact as a constitutional signpost pointing toward the elimination of all kinds of legal barriers based on race and as a landmark from which broad changes in black-white relations can be dated. It reflected a subtle trend of constitutional adjudication, an indication of an attitude by the Supreme Court to focus on issues before it in a different way than prior courts had done.[11]

In deciding *Brown,* the Court cut through the fiction surrounding the old "separate but equal" doctrine to the realities which had always been patently obvious to all who were willing to see: that "separate" could never be "equal," because its very genesis and its only purpose for being was to be invidiously discriminatory, to keep the black man in an inferior status.[12] But self-evident as this has always been, it was not until 1954—just twenty years ago and almost one hundred years after the adoption of the thirteenth, fourteenth and fifteenth amendments—that the Court was willing to accord a full constitutional recognition and significance to this unmistakable reality.

The willingness to look at the real impact of governmental action, to search for truth amid the fictions of legal doctrine, brought a new freshness to constitutional adjudication, a recognition that the basic law must be willing to grapple with everyday reality. This is why the Warren Court became a place of particular promise and hope for black people, who were thereby encouraged to believe that racial justice is actually attainable, that the law could understand their own reality in a way which would allow it to frame meaningful relief from the everyday denials of constitutional principle and right.[13] The stifling of this new realism by division in the Supreme Court or by cutting back on *Brown* would set back the great goal of equal justice under law.

I conclude by making this appeal:

To adherents of civil rights who have become discouraged and cynical, I say that this is not the time for the summer soldier or the sunshine patriot. The road ahead in the march for equality, in law and in fact, is filled with great obstacles difficult to surmount. But we must persevere if we are to bring the full blessings of freedom and equality to us and to our posterity.

Therefore, it is imperative that those who genuinely believe in civil rights persist in their efforts with courage and fortitude. Racial segregation and discrimination continue, but it is lesser in degree than when *Brown* was decided. This no one can deny.

True, the pace for total elimination of racial discrimination has been with all too deliberate speed.[14] But the Supreme Court itself has abandoned this concept. Today the constitutional mandate for equality is for the here and now and not a mere promise for the indefinite future.[15]

Furthermore, the areas of denial of civil rights encompass important areas in addition to education, such as jobs, housing, voting, criminal and civil justice and accommodations that are public in fact although private in form. The elimination of racial barriers against equality in these aspects of American life simply is too important to permit cynicism, discouragement or half-hearted dedication to rectifying injustice.

I also appeal to the coalition of civil rights adherents, splintered in the *DeFunis* case, not to engage in acrimony, but to seek to restore the prior unity which existed, not by compromise—because compromise of constitutional principles is impermissible—but by returning to a common program of seeking to eliminate racial discrimination by supporting realistic remedies rather than submitting to ill-founded fears.

It would be presumptuous for me to appeal to the Supreme Court. I can only express the hope that the Court will unite as it did during the Warren era in support of that concept nobly expressed on the great edifice which houses the Court: Equal Justice For All.

And, finally, I also express the hope that the people of this country will abjure prejudice, fear and hate and will apply and practice the teachings of our common Judaic-Christian tradition, that all men are God's children, created in His image.

In *Brown*, the Court did its duty, under circumstances reminiscent of an earlier decision of the Supreme Court, *Worcester v. Georgia*,[16] decided in 1832. In that case, the Supreme Court upheld the claim of the Cherokee Indians to treaty land against annexation by the State of Georgia. This ruling aroused great anger on the part of President Jackson and Georgia. There were rumors and even threats that both the President and Georgia would decline to follow the Court's decision. Referring to these reports, Justice Story, in a letter to a friend, said this:

> Georgia is full of anger and violence. What she will do, it is difficult to say. Probably she will resist the execution of our judgment, and if she does, I do not believe the President will interfere. ... The rumor is, that he has told the Georgians he will do nothing. I, for one, feel quite easy on this subject, be the event what it may. The Court has done its duty. Let the Nation now do theirs.[17]

In May of 1954, the Court in *Brown* did its duty. Now, in 1974 and in the years to come, let both the present Court and the Nation do theirs by fulfilling the still-unrealized American creed that all men are created free and equal.

---

[1] 347 U.S. 483 (1954).

[2] Twenty years ago, many groups united with the N.A.A.C.P. in urging the Court to take this "great civilizing step" of overturning the "separate but equal" principle of *Plessy v. Ferguson*. This coalition included the federal government, represented by the Justice Department; Jewish organizations, such as the American Jewish Congress; labor groups such as the American Federation of Teachers and the Congress of Industrial Organizations; defenders of civil rights such as the American Civil Liberties Union and the American Council on Human Rights, and other interested groups such as the American Veterans Committee. See *Bolling v. Sharp*, 347 U.S. 497, 498 (1954); *Brown v. Board of Education*, 347 U.S. 483, 485-86 (1954).

[3] The fallout from the coalition that helped bring *Brown* about is evidenced by the briefs in the pending Supreme Court case of *DeFunis v. Odegaard*. No. 73-235. The American Jewish Congress, the American Jewish Committee, the Anti-Defamation League, the AFL-CIO and other groups generally supportive of civil rights filed amici briefs in support of DeFunis.

On the other hand, Jewish organizations, such as the National Council of Jewish Women and the Union of Hebrew Congregations; union groups such as the United Farm Workers, United Auto Workers, United Mine Workers, and State, County and Municipal Employees; The Lawyers' Committee for Civil Rights Under Law; the National Education Association; the Children's Defense Fund; the ACLU; the N.A.A.C.P.; the Legal Defense Fund and other important organizations have filed briefs in support of the disputed program of the Law School of Washington. The Equal Employment Opportunity Commission filed a motion supported by a brief amicus curiae in support of the program, but Solicitor General Bork disavowed this brief for the government and upon his application the Supreme Court rejected it.

[4] It is in these terms that the issue has been phrased in some of the briefs filed in *DeFunis*. See Brief of the Anti-Defamation League at 2 (question is: Whether a state may establish a racial quota).

[5] See *Brown v. Board of Education*, 347 U.S. 483, 485 (1954). The importance of the admission of the minority student to an integrated legal classroom was recognized even before *Brown*. In 1950, the Court in *Sweatt v. Painter* held that the education that a black student could receive at a law school established for blacks could never be equal to the legal education at the University of Texas Law School. 339 U.S. 629 (1950). To the Court, the fact that the ostensibly objective facilities were equivalent

was not controlling. As Chief Justice Vinson stated:

> What is more important, the University of Texas Law School possesses to a far greater degree those qualities which are incapable of objective measurement but which make for greatness in a law school. Such qualities include reputation of the faculty, experience of the administration, position and influence of the alumni, standing in the community, traditions, and prestige.

[6] *Id.* at 634.

[6] See *Milliken v. Bradley,* cert. granted Nov. 19, 1973, 42 U.S.L.W. 3306 (U.S. Nov. 20, 1973) Nos. 73-434, 73-435, 73-436 (geographic boundaries); *Gonzales v. Fairfax-Brewster Schools, Inc.,* 363 F. Supp. 1200 (E.D. Va. 1973), appeal docketed, No. 73-2351 (4th Cir. Nov. 13, 1973) (desegregation of private school under U.S.C. section 1981).

[7] 347 U.S. 483 (1954).

[8] I use this term to designate the chronological period during which Earl Warren was Chief Justice of the United States and the term "the Burger Court" to designate the present Court.

[9] See, *e.g., Green v. County School Board,* 391 U.S. 430 (1968); *Griffin v. Board of Education,* 377 U.S. 218 (1964); *Goss v. Board of Education,* 373 U.S. 683 (1963); *Cooper v. Aaron,* 358 U.S. 1 (1958). The Burger Court has been able to remain unanimous on certain issues. See *Swann v. Board of Education,* 402 U.S. 1 (1971); *Alexander v. Board of Education,* 396 U.S. 19 (1969).

[10] In *Wright v. Council of City of Emporia,* the Court split 5-4 on whether a municipality can break off from an existing school district which has not yet completed the process of dismantling a system of enforced racial segregation. 407 U.S. 451 (1972). The Court in *Carter v. West Feliciana Parish School Board,* while concurring in result, disagreed as to the proper timetable for the implementation of a court-ordered pupil transfer plan. 396 U.S. 290 (1970). And in two important desegregation cases last term, the Court also divided. In *Keyes v. School District No. 1,* Justice Rehnquist dissented, while Justices Douglas and Powell wrote concurring opinions. 413 U.S. 189 (1973). In *Bradley v. School Board,* the Court, with Justice Powell not participating, affirmed by an equally divided vote, a lower court holding disallowing a desegregation plan which crossed county lines. 412 U.S. 92 (1973).

[11] A. GOLDBERG, EQUAL JUSTICE 22 (1971).

[12] *Id.* at 21.

[13] *Id.* at 23.

[14] *Brown v. Board of Education,* 349 U.S. 294, 301 (1955).

[15] *Watson v. City of Memphis,* 373 U.S. 526, 533 (1963).

[16] 31 U.S. (6 Pet.) 515 (1832).

[17] 1 C. WARREN, THE SUPREME COURT IN UNITED STATES HISTORY, (1926).

The Message of *Brown* for White America

Theodore M. Hesburgh, C.S.C.

Much has been said at this Conference about the progress of black Americans since the *Brown* decision 20 years ago. I would like to concentrate for a while, however, on white Americans, another segment of the population which has benefited tremendously from the changes wrought by the decision. *Brown v. Board of Education* began the long, hard, and unfinished process by which American laws and practices are being brought into line with the mandate for racial equality that is the Fourteenth Amendment. Yet *Brown's* promise of full equality remains as a great challenge to white America.

I am mindful of another time of great disturbance and great unrest and challenge when solutions to our racial problems seemed almost out of reach. The great liberator, Abraham Lincoln, went to Gettysburg, that bloody battlefield of hatred and war, and in simple words told Americans to be what God had called them to be, to create the nation that had been born of such promise, to be worthy of these blessings and to do what only they could do. He said it briefly. And it seems to me in reflecting on all the personal efforts that have gone into the Civil Rights movement over so many years, over so many dusty roads, over so many obstacles that seemed insurmountable, that we can't stop here. We must make a living document of our lives so that all of us, in our own ways, and in our own lives, and our own circles, can make equal justice and equality of opportunity a reality in our time.

White Americans in a Pluralistic Society

Over the twenty years since *Brown*, white Americans have begun to face the critical challenge of realizing that they exist in a pluralistic society—a

81

society in which no group can be secure unless all groups are afforded equal opportunity and respect. And in many ways, particularly in the 1960s, white Americans have met that challenge. Largely gone are the "white only" laws and institutions which dictated an apartheid society and which belittled the dignity of the oppressor as much as that of the oppressed. White Americans can point with pride to the fact that our government is the only one to meet the challenge of large-scale racial diversity head-on and affirm the principle that all men are created equal. On an individual level, many white Americans have been forced to come to grips with their own deep-seated racism and, in many cases, that racism has been replaced by enlightenment and understanding. And as a result of the greater acceptance and appreciation for the contribution of minority groups, white Americans have been immeasurably enriched.

But just as there is still a long way to go before racial justice is achieved for blacks and other minorities, for whites too there is a tremendous challenge and a tremendous opportunity to fulfill the destiny of this country. As W.E.B. DuBois said at the beginning of this century, "The problem of the 20th century is the problem of the color line." That remains our number one problem today. Now, even more than when DuBois wrote those words the future of our nation may depend on achieving full racial justice at last.

The importance of our educational process for the future of racial justice in America cannot be overestimated. I believe that education is the key to future racial harmony. In the *Brown* case, the Supreme Court told us that to separate black children solely because of their race "may affect their hearts and minds in a way unlikely ever to be undone." I believe that white children and white adults, who grow up and go through life separated from persons of other races, also have their hearts and minds affected in ways unlikely ever to be undone. We do damage to their hearts and minds when we educate children merely to be successful in an apartheid society, or in artifically segregated areas of a society. We do damage when we raise our children in an educational incubator where they develop false notions of racial and cultural superiority. We do damage when we shield white children from the fact that one out of every six Americans is a member of a racial minority. We do damage when we fail to inform white children that eighty percent of the world's population is non-white.

It is foolish to think we can ignore the racial, ethnic and cultural diversity in American society and in the world; and it is absurd to bring children up in an educational system which ignores it.

There is mounting evidence that white students suffer educational and psychic damage from segregated schooling. Dr. Kenneth Clark, the eminent psychologist whose studies were relied upon by the Supreme Court in the *Brown* decision has written: "There is strong evidence to suggest that racial segregation is detrimental to privileged middle class and to working class white children. Segregated schools and cruelty in American ghettos are deadening and destroying the ethical and personal and human effectiveness of American white children." It is readily apparent to any observer of the American scene during the past five years that white students appear to be suffering from frustration at their inability to reconcile the sharp divisions between white and black, between Anglo and Latino, between rich and poor, and between American ideals and American reality. As Kenneth Keniston, a Yale psychologist and member of the Advisory Council of the Center for Civil Rights has written: "It does not take a psychologist to emphasize that the causes of student protest lie not only in the psyches of the students, but even more, in the world we inhabit. The shameful legacy of racism, America's dubious imperial role in the world, the inertia and compromise of our universities—these are simple facts against which the ethical impulse of the young is directed." We cannot afford to allow American education to continue to fail white as well as black children. We must ensure that the ethical impulse of the young is nurtured in an environment that includes the full range of racial, ethnic, and social diversity that makes up our nation.

If we fail to establish that integrated, pluralistic environment for our children and ourselves it will not be blacks alone who lose, it will be the majority white part of this nation who will be deprived of that richness that is the black culture around us and the black warmth and the black friendship. How many whites have missed this heritage which is peculiarly ours as a nation, and how many are poorer for it? The great pluralism of America is simply wasted when we break up into little water tight ghettoes, whether it be the ghetto of South Chicago or the ghetto of Puerto Rican New York, or even the white ghetto of Notre Dame for so many years. Our all-white suburbs are just as much "ghettoes." These ghettoes are the islands where whites harbor distorted views of their fellow Americans. And, increasingly, because of the nation's failure to solve its racial problems, these are the islands where many white Americans live in fear and apprehension. It is obvious that white Americans suffer when this society is divided into separate, unequal, and alien groups. White Americans suffer when this society is torn by violence. And all Americans suffer when we co-exist in an uneasy peace purchased at the cost of repressive action.

We must all break up these ghettos, we must all somehow reach out and embrace the total pluralism that is America. We must do so not by homogenizing it, but by letting each part of America mutually enrich the others so that we are all enriched in the process and justice is achieved. Then each person can stand tall in dignity and say "I am a human being. I am made in the image and likeness of God, and I can live accordingly."

The *Brown* decision freed this country from the unjust and immoral "separate but equal" doctrine approved by the Supreme Court in the 1896 case of *Plessy v. Ferguson.* This decision contained a prophetic dissent by the first Justice Harlan: "The destinies of the two races, in this country, are indissoluably linked together." I believe that the destiny of this nation lies in achieving effective racial integration.

The Need for Racial Harmony

Now, more than ever, white Americans must adjust to the inevitable changes in American society which will be necessary to foster and maintain racial harmony. While we have come a long way, the way ahead also is difficult. The simple problems are behind us and the most complex ones loom ahead. The solution to the problems of racial injustice which we face today must be the nation's first priority. These problems cannot be swept under the rug, and we must not be distracted by other pursuits.

The present is very much a time for the "winter soldiers" of the civil rights movement to carry forward the struggle. While the fevered intensity of the sixties has cooled and there is precious little recognition in the movement anymore, those whose commitment to racial justice is more than just a passing fancy, must now make their presence felt. Until we have achieved racial and economic justice in this country, neither black nor white, red nor brown can be at peace in the community or in his soul.

In speaking of the responsibilities of white America in general, it would be myopic of me to overlook the responsibilities of whites at this university. For most of our existence we have been an exclusively male and almost exclusively white institution. But times are changing and this institution must change as rapidly, if not more so, than the rest of society.

The establishment of the Center for Civil Rights at Notre Dame reaffirms this university's commitment to the struggle for what should be in this country and in the world. But we must not permit a gap between our larger goals and the realities here at home. This university must be a model for a successfully integrated society. It is not enough that we seek to become this model with "all deliberate speed." We must do so now. This is my commitment and it must be the commitment of the university.

Let us rededicate ourselves to make the dream of equality come true. While we realize that in the twenty years that have passed since the *Brown* decision many great things have happened, there is so much more yet to do and so far yet to go. We must keep moving forward. In those wonderful words of Robert Frost, although the woods, in this case, may be unlovely and dark and deep, we all know that we have promises to keep and miles to go before we sleep. God bless you all and bring you home safely.

Bibliography

Blackwell, Randolph T., "Perspective on the *Brown* Decision," *New South,* 28(Winter, 1973) 9-17.

Clotfelter, Charles T., "Twenty Years After the *Brown* Decision: Does Integration Have a Future?" *Harvard Crimson,* May 21, 1974.

Cox, Archibald, "After Twenty Years. Reflections Upon the Constitutional Significance of *Brown v. Board of Education" Civil Rights Digest,* 6(Summer, 1974) 38-45.

Dewar, Helen, "Prince Edward County: Paying for 'Massive Resistance'," *Washington Post,* May 12, 1974.

Edelman, Marian Wright, *Twenty Years After "Brown": Where Are We Now?* April 4, 1974. ERIC ED 094 015.

Feinberg, Lawrence, "Washington's Way: From Integration to a Black System, *Washington Post,* May 12, 1974 [District of Columbia].

Fiss, Owen M., "The Fate of An Idea Whose Time Has Come: Antidiscrimination Law in the Second Decade after *Brown v. Board of Education," University of Chicago Law Review* 41 (Summer 1974) 742-773.

Grieder, William, "Winners and Losers," *Race Relations Reporter,* 5(May, 1974) 19-22 [Summerton, S.C.].

Hesburgh, Theodore M., "Civil Rights: Old Victories, New Battles," *The Nation,* 219 (September 14, 1974) 207-210.

Hesburgh, Theodore M., "Preface: Fiftieth Anniversary Volume," *Notre Dame Lawyer,* 50 (October, 1974) 6-16.

Peterson, Franklynn, "The School Desegregation Case That Started It All," *Dallas News,* January 20, 1974 [Topeka].

Poinsett, Alex, "Whatever Happened to School Desegregation?" *Ebony,* 29(May, 1974) 104-114.

Scott, Austin, "Topeka Treadmill: Linda Brown's City Faces a New Battle," *Washington Post,* May 12, 1974.

Ward, Francis, "Historic School Desegregation Case Still Open," *Los Angeles Times,* May 13, 1974 [Topeka].

Wright, J. Skelly, "Promises to Keep," *Integrated Education,* 12(September-October, 1974) 3-8.